VISITO...
PEAK ...STRICT

LINDSEY PORTER

MPC

Published by:
Moorland Publishing Co Ltd,
Moor Farm Road West, Ashbourne,
Derbyshire DE6 1HD England

ISBN 0 86190 515 6

1st edition 1982
2nd edition 1984
3rd edition 1989
4th revised and redesigned edition 1994
Reprinted 1995

British Library Cataloguing in Publication Data:
A catalogue record for this book is available from the British Library.

Colour origination by: DP Graphics, Wiltshire

Printed in the Hong Kong by: Wing King Tong Co Ltd

Front cover: Crag Hall
Rear Cover: Well dressing at Tissington
Title page: Rock climbing on Stanage Edge
All illustrations, including cover, are from the MPC Picture Collection.

MPC Production Team
Editorial and Design: John Robey
Cartography: Alastair Morrison

CONTENTS

Key to Symbols Used in Text Margin and on Maps

⌂ Church	ℹ Tourist Information
Castle	✳ Other Place of Interest
Building of Interest	Nature Reserve
Museum/Art Gallery	Garden
Industrial Archaeology	Beautiful View/Natural Phenomenon
Interesting Railway	Park/Country Park
Archaeological Site	Cave/Mine

Key to Maps

▬▬ Main Road	City/Town
▬▬ Secondary Road	◯ Town/Village
▬▬ Minor Road	River/Lake
Other Tracks	⋯⋯ Peak Park Boundary
	⋯⋯ County Boundary

How To Use This Guide

This MPC Visitor's Guide has been designed to be as easy to use as possible. Each chapter covers a region and gives all the background information to help you enjoy your visit. MPC's distinctive margin symbols, the important places printed in bold and a comprehensive index enable the reader to find the most interesting places to visit with ease.

At the end of each chapter an Additional Information section gives specific details such as addresses and opening times, making this guide a complete sightseeing companion.

At the back of the guide the Fact File, arranged in alphabetical order, gives practical information and useful tips to help you plan your holiday before you go and while you are there.

The maps of each region show the main towns, villages, roads and places of interest, but are not designed as route maps and motorists should always use a good recommended road atlas.

INTRODUCTION

In recent years there has been a marked increase in the number of publications on the Peak District, some of doubtful accuracy. Why then this one? Despite this wealth of literature, there is no one publication which aims to aid the visitor by offering advice as to how to make the most of a visit or holiday in the area. This book tries to fill that gap, but it is not, of course, entirely comprehensive. For one thing, commercial considerations dictate what is available and new attractions occur each season. There is also the question of taste and preference and, of equal importance, the fact that the author is a local historian rather than a naturalist. There is still room for a rambler's guide to the area written by a natural historian, but this may mean identifying the localities of rare species and may cause a conflict of interests.

The Peak District lies at the southern end of the Pennines surrounded by the cities of Sheffield to the north-east, Manchester to the north-west, Stoke-on-Trent to the south-west and Derby to the south-east. Although the Peak is often regarded as being wholly in Derbyshire it must be remembered that large areas to the west are in Staffordshire — indeed Dovedale is the county boundary here and some of the most spectacular scenery is on the Staffordshire bank — while west of Buxton a significant area of the Peak lies in Cheshire, with some areas to the north in South Yorkshire.

The rich diversity of scenery has long been an attraction for visitors, sufficient to move the hearts and pens of many nationally-known writers over the centuries. Nowadays, for convenience, the area is often sub-divided into the White Peak and the Dark Peak, each with its own quite distinct character.

The White Peak, defined very approximately as the countryside enclosed by the towns of Buxton, Castleton, Bakewell, Matlock and Ashbourne, is a limestone plateau of green fields and white stone walls. This upland is dissected by the rivers Derwent, Wye, Dove, Manifold and their tributaries to give the region's well-known dales, some with spectacular limestone rocks and cliffs. Dovedale, Manifold Valley, Chee Dale, Monsal Dale, Lathkill Dale and the Matlock Gorge are all deservedly popular beauty spots, while there are many more lesser known dales, many now 'dry' without their rippling trout streams, which are a delight to explore.

To the north and along the eastern and western margins of this limestone plateau lies the Dark Peak — upland areas of grassland, with moorlands covered with heather, bilberry and cotton grass, growing on gritstone and shale with a peaty acid soil, often a less hospitable area left to the sheep and grouse. This is the country loved by the rambler who wishes to 'get away from it all' and the rock gymnasts who delight in scaling the numerous gritstone 'edges'. But even this area is served by many minor roads, so that the less energetic can park easily and take a gentle stroll along the top of one of the edges with magnificent views over the surrounding country-side.

Couple all this with a rich historical background of stately homes, show caves, ancient lead mines, picturesque watermills, a network of old packhorse ways and numerous small towns and villages to explore, then it becomes clear why the Peak District is the most visited (some would say over-used) national park in the western world.

Over-usage of places such as Dovedale, the Pennine Way path over Kinder Scout and Stanage Edge is causing, or has caused, erosion and the degeneration of paths to a point at which they are no longer acceptable to many visitors. If this book succeeds in its aim of making visitors aware that there are other areas of equal importance and attractiveness, then its publication will be justified. The thing most country-lovers seek, or seem to seek, is fine rural surroundings accompanied by a certain degree of solitude. One cannot over stress that there are so many areas in the Peak where this can be achieved if one looks beyond such beauty spots as Dovedale.

Throughout this book mention is made of the OS map, or Ordnance Survey Map to give its full title, and Grid Reference numbers. It is essential to carry the maps called 'The White Peak' and 'The Dark Peak'. They contain such a wealth of information for visitors that they are indispensable. Do not be put off by thinking that you cannot read a map, for a little practice will show you how easy it really is.

A look at an atlas will show vividly the point made above relating to the geographical location of the Peak District National Park. It is unique in that its 555sq miles are surrounded by one conurbation after another. In fact, over 17½ million people live with 50 miles of the region and the Park attracts 2.2 million visitors per year. But this book is not confined to a study of the Park itself. There are large areas of interest which are beyond its boundaries, but are included here; the Churnet Valley is a specific example.

The Peak District National Park came into being as a result of the *National Parks and Access to the Countryside Act* of 1949. This was a result of pressure brought to bear on politicians, but its grass roots and geographical base was the Peak District. The National Park which became established differed from others (except the Lake District) in that it was vested with control over planning matters as well as having responsibility for providing information services to visitors. The policies of the Peak Park Joint Planning Board (referred to hereafter as the National Park) often conflict with the pressures of society, particularly industry, and restrictions on residential development have contributed to high property prices. This, combined with other important factors, eg decline in the economic importance of agriculture in the upland areas, has resulted in a gradual depopulation of rural communities, particularly among young people. This vicious circle then makes schools redundant, and young people seek a life amongst their own age group in towns. There is no easy solution to this and on balance one has to admit that the establishment of the National Park came just at the right time and that its policies have been to our advantage. The Board's vision statement: 'caring for a living landscape' sums up well its role.

The National Park also produces a considerable amount of literature on the area, much of it being for schools and some of it in French, Italian, Dutch and German. These leaflets are quite useful and informative to more than schoolchildren and can be obtained directly from the National Park at Bakewell or from its information centres, including its mobile caravan which can be found at agricultural shows, etc. Among the wealth of other publications, four books stand out, being based upon original research and comprehensive in their approach. They are *The Peak District* by Millward and Robinson (Eyre Methuen); *The Peak District* by Edwards in the New Naturalist series, now a Fontana paperback; *Peakland Roads and Trackways* by A. E. & E. M. Dodd and *Wild Flowers and other plants of the Peak District* by Anderson and Shimwell. However, the majority of these books are now out of print. There are of course definitive books on other

The Peak District has many remains of its prehistoric inhabitants — Arbor Low stone circle, near Monyash

The remains of an ancient coral reef — Parkhouse Hill and the Sugar Loaf in the Upper Dove Valley

Peak variety: (above) vernacular architecture at Bakewell's Old House Museum; (below) a grander building at the Stables, Chatsworth

disciplines such as geology, but these books are recommended for a good general background to the area. There are plenty of walkers' guides to the Peak District, including one by this author. An attempt has been made to include a fair selection of walks in this book, which can easily be extended or shortened to suit particular needs using the OS map and following other rights of way. The 2½in or 1:50,000 scale maps show every field and with the whole of the Peak almost entirely on two maps it is possible to sort out all manner of routes with comparative ease.

The Peak has been crossed by a countless number of old roads and packhorse ways which have now degenerated to bridlepaths or footpaths. This is an important legacy which we are most fortunate to have. It means that we can leave the car and really get to know an area on paths now little used.

Such is the network of paths that in some areas there is no difficulty in finding circular routes in order to return to the car. Good parking areas are provided in many places and are marked on the White Peak OS map. At this point perhaps one should stress a word of warning. These maps indicate quite readily just how proliferous are the old lead mines in the area. They present few problems to the rambler so long as they are avoided. On no account enter mine workings or caves without an expert, or remove the stones capping a shaft, or for that matter, climb rock faces. The caving and mountain rescue posts were not established without good reason and a memorial at Castleton Youth Hostel to Neil Moss is a reminder that all who go underground do not necessarily return. Rock faces and the northern moors have also claimed their share of lives; it is all a case of being sensible.

Finally, please remember that when the visitor has gone home the local has to live and work in the Peak. Respect his property and privacy, his animals and crops and remember the adage: 'leave only footprints, take only photographs'; and have an enjoyable time.

The Role of the National Park

With 22 million day visits a year, the Peak National Park is said to be the second most-visited in the world, next to Mount Fuji in Japan. This staggering number of visitors poses serious problems for The Peak National Park authority, whose job it is to conserve and enhance the landscape while providing quiet, open-air recreational opportunities for those who come to enjoy it.

Traffic jams in the popular villages every summer weekend, worn-out or eroded footpaths and queues for all the major attractions are all manifestations of the Peak's perennial popularity. It is the National Park authority's job to try to balance the often conflicting interests of conservation and recreation, and over the years, it has come up with several innovative and award-winning schemes to achieve this.

Examples are the Tissington, High Peak and Monsal Trails — unsightly and derelict former railway lines which have been converted by the National Park to pleasant walking and cycling routes with associated car parks and picnic areas. These railway trails give easy, traffic-free access to the beautiful White Peak landscape, and the Routes for People scheme in the 1970s was an attempt to provide different routes for different users in the same area.

In the Dark Peak area, separating visitors from traffic was more difficult, but the Peak pioneered one of the first road closure and traffic management schemes in Britain in the Goyt Valley in 1970. The popular valley road was closed to traffic at busy weekends, and a minibus service provided for those who could not or would not walk.

A similar traffic management scheme was set up by the Park authority and partners in the Upper Derwent Valley in 1981, with minibus, cycle hire, car parks and information provision. This scheme has won awards for its effective linking of conservation and recreation objectives in a valley visited by 1.25 million people every year.

Another practical way in which the Park authority has tried to ease the congestion problem on the narrow roads of the Park is by subsidising public transport routes by train and bus, encouraging people to leave their cars at home.

Although the National Park authority is not the statutory footpath authority in the area, the Ranger Service is often involved in restoration work on the most badly-eroded footpaths. Teams of conservation volunteers, supervised by rangers, are out almost every weekend engaged on this work, and a full-time team of five are exclusively employed in restoring the Pennine Way — one of the most seriously eroded footpaths in Britain.

Despite the popularity of the National Park there are many areas of the Peak District where, even on a busy Bank Holiday, you can get away from the crowds. Like most areas of countryside the Peak needs to be explored on foot, and many of the walks recommended in this guide enable you to enjoy the great variety of landscapes in what many regard as the most interesting of Britain's national parks.

Tissington is a village popular with visitors

Part of the region's historical legacy: the Riley Graves (which contain the Hancock family), who all died in August 1666, victims of the Eyam Plague

*Many come to the Peak District to experience 'the Great Outdoors' —
Curbar Edge*

1
THE SOUTHWEST

The south-western edge of the Peak District is an area of open and often treeless moorland dissected by three river systems — the Churnet, Dane and Goyt. Flowing off the high moors, these three major valleys offer good walking, extensive views and considerable pleasure. There is also much to see. The huge outcrops of rocks known as the Roaches are perhaps the most notable geographical feature. Man has however added much else — the reservoirs of the Goyt and at Tittesworth, interesting market towns, preserved mills and the majestic Tudor Gothic mansion of Alton Towers. One is tempted to single out particular parts of the valleys for special comment, but this would perhaps be misleading for all three are very attractive in their own particular way. There are no contrasting features like those found in the valleys of the Dove and Manifold, for instance, where sandstones and shales give way to the harder limestone. Here, all the rocks are different varieties of sandstone and shales. It is therefore a different kind of topography moulded in softer rock than the limestone, creating rugged heather and bilberry clad moors in the upper valleys. Further downstream, wooded and often deep, wide valleys are more characteristic.

The Churnet rises to the east of the Roaches and Ramshaw Rocks, flowing into Tittesworth Reservoir. Standing on the road bridge at Meerbrook, over the northern end of Tittesworth Reservoir, the water looks like a huge mirror for the Roaches escarpment behind. The Roaches and Windgather Rocks have been used by climbers for a long time and the recent purchase of the former by the National Park has secured access to the rock faces, which are numerous, with various grades of severity.

To the east rises the ridge known as Morridge, with the Mermaid

Inn standing out on the treeless skyline. Just to the north of the inn is Blakemere, more popularly known as the Mermaid Pool, traditionally said to be bottomless and the home of a mermaid. It is strange that a pool very similar to this and known as Doxey Pool also exists on the Roaches. The inn was on an old drover's road that ran from Cheshire into the Peak District via Hartington and Newhaven. There is only limited parking on the narrow road which runs beneath the Roaches. However there is now a free park-and-ride scheme which operates from Tittesworth Reservoir at weekends. Vehicles are left at the Meerbrook end, where there is a visitor centre close to the Meerbrook-Blackshaw Moor road. There is also a café and some facilities for children.

The Axe Edge moors afford good views over quite a large area. From the layby just south of the Mermaid Inn on Morridge one can, for instance, see to the Welsh Hills and the Wrekin in Shropshire on a clear day. The more immediate view down to the Roaches and Ramshaw Rocks is perhaps more spectacular. If your route takes you up the Leek-Buxton road past Ramshaw Rocks, drive slowly looking for the rock which obviously resembles a face. It is known as the Winking Eye rock and it does just that as you drive past it.

Below Tittesworth Reservoir, the river skirts the old market town of Leek. The water has for centuries been used for power and for its very pure qualities. The Cistercian monks built one of the largest abbey churches of their order in England on the banks of the River Churnet at Abbey Green, Leek and also established a watermill, presumably to grind corn. The abbey is no more, but a preserved cornmill still stands on the site of the original mill.

At Leek, the river sweeps in a huge arc around the town, meandering out almost to Rudyard where it flows back towards the town in a very deep valley carved out by overflow waters from a glacial lake, known as Lake Dane, that was situated just to the north of Rudyard Lake. A good place to view this is from the Leek to Stoke-on-Trent road (the A53) where it crosses the river. Below Cheddleton, where another preserved watermill exists, the valley is well wooded and remains so almost to Alton village where it becomes shallower. This section is perhaps the prettiest part of the valley, but it is often neglected by visitors to the Peak District. The reason for this is the lack of roads which keep the motorcar away. It is still traversed by its railway and canal and the latter adds to the tranquil atmosphere.

The valley of the River Dane is similar to the Churnet in that motor traffic is denied access to much of it. The river rises on Axe Edge above Three Shires Head and flows roughly westwards to the

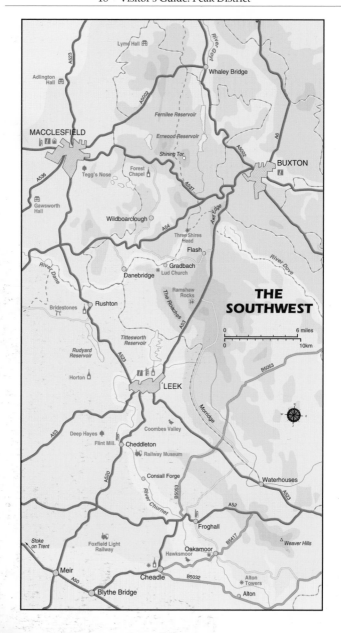

Cheshire plain where it meanders slowly towards the River Weaver. It has a tributary, the Clough Brook which collects the waters from the Wildboarclough district, and is another large and beautiful valley or 'clough' worth exploring.

The valleys of the Dane and Clough Brook were important to the laden packhorses which crossed the southern Pennines carrying salt to the east of England. An interesting feature of Three Shires Head — where the counties of Cheshire, Derbyshire and Staffordshire meet — are the many packhorse routes which converge on Panniers Pool Bridge, now the exclusive preserve of the rambler.

Lower downstream near Gradbach a huge landslip has created a gorge of considerable proportions high on the hillside. It is known as Lud Church and is well worth the effort of getting to it. In excess of 50ft deep and in places only a few feet wide, it became a meeting

Autumn in the Churnet Valley near Oakamoor

place of religious dissenters some 500 years ago and supposedly takes its name from their leader. Above Lud Church and Back Forest in which it is situated, various paths cut through the heather and bilberry amid the exposed gritstone rock. This is the home of the grouse and curlew, disturbed only by the rambler enjoying the magnificent scenery. Below Danebridge, where a road crosses the valley and makes a good starting place to explore the area, the valley is the preserve of the rambler again. After a few miles it widens out and ends abruptly under the shadow of Bosley Cloud, a huge out-crop of harder gritstones.

The Goyt starts close to the Dane in the wide expanse of peat bogs north of Three Shires Head. Once the tree line is reached the valley becomes of more interest but its physical character is lost beneath the waters of Fernilee and Errwood reservoirs. To the west rises Shining Tor and the exposed edge of gritstone known as Windgather Rocks. There is however plenty of interest in the Goyt valley despite much of it being flooded.

Compared with other areas of the Peak, there is not a great deal remaining of early occupation in this area. A notable exception is the prehistoric burial mound known as the Bridestones, situated at the southern end of the large hill known as Bosley Cloud close to the Congleton-Rushton-Leek road. It is a chambered burial tomb with some very tall standing stones. It is visible from the road, accessible to the public and well worth examining. The road which passes it is part of the Earls Way — an old route from the Earl of Chester's land in Cheshire to Dieulacresse Abbey at Leek (founded by an Earl of Chester) and his properties east of the town — and is at least medieval in origin. While parked by the Bridestones, look out to the west. On a clear day one can see the Welsh Hills and much nearer, Jodrell Bank Radio Telescope, in Cheshire.

Dieulacresse Abbey at Leek has been completely destroyed, ex-cept for a small part of a pillar and is in any case on private ground, but of comparable age is the town's parish church which is well worth a visit. The parish church of St Edward the Confessor at Leek is on a very ancient site for it was founded in 1042. It has a beautiful pair of thirteenth-century rose windows, a ducking stool and ancient crosses in the churchyard. Despite alterations over a thousand years much of interest remains of the old church. A guide book is on sale at the church.

Two further churches of similar age to Leek are Cheddleton and Horton, situated about 4 miles south and west of Leek respectively. Further north Rushton church, chiefly built of stone and wood and situated in the fields halfway between Rushton James and Rushton Spencer to serve both villages, is well worth a visit. Two further churches are noteworthy. North of Wildboarclough is Forest Chapel erected in 1673 and rebuilt in 1834, where the annual rush laying ceremony can be observed. The other is the Roman Catholic Church at Cheadle, Staffordshire, which was built during 1840-6 and is considered to be the finest Victorian Gothic church in the country. It was designed by A. W. N. Pugin while enjoying the patronage and friendship of the Earl of Shrewsbury who paid out some £40,000 for it. It is incongruously situated off the main street, its huge spire overshadowing the town. But its richly painted interior is a not-to-be-overlooked 'must' for many visitors.

There are several houses of considerable antiquity in the district. Most are not open to the public, but in some cases a footpath passes quite near. For instance, there are Whitehough and Sharpcliffe Hall between Leek and Ipstones, Wincle Grange near Wincle, the remains of the Norman castle near Alton, and the delightful Gawsworth Hall, which may be visited.

The Churnet Valley

The water of the valley gave rise to textile industries which developed to take advantage of its power and purity. **Leek** developed as a textile town producing silk. The pure water of the Churnet gave rise to the development of the dyeing industry. This grew particularly in the nineteenth century when it was found that the water could be used to produce the raven-black dyes for which the town became so famous and which were so popular with the Victorians. Old textile mills mingle with silk workers' houses, but none are open to the public, although various 'mill shops' sell garments: slacks, ladies' nightwear and underwear, etc.

A walk around Leek's main streets reveals the Victorian influence particularly under the design of the Sugdens, a local firm of architects. The town's cornmill in Mill Street has been preserved and is worth a visit. It is claimed by the enthusiasts to have been built by James Brindley, who had his workshops in the town. The waterwheel and all its machinery are intact and in working condition and the second floor has been developed as a museum to Brindley. Although better known as a canal engineer, his early career was as a millwright and he had close ties with the town.

An interesting phenomenon is sometimes observed from the churchyard from the 20- 22 June each year. At this time, if conditions are satisfactory, the setting sun can be seen to set behind Bosley Cloud completely, only to re-appear and finally set over the Cheshire plain. The double sunset can never be guaranteed, but many go to watch this spectacle each year.

Visitors are welcome at the Coombes Valley Nature Reserve, which protects woodland and pasture in the Coombes Valley, a tributary of the Churnet, between Cheddleton and Ipstones near to Leek. The Hawksmore Nature Reserve near Oakamoor, on the road to Cheadle also welcomes visitors. It is owned by the National Trust and a trail has been laid out in the extensive grounds which drop towards the Churnet.

At **Cheddleton** on the A520 south of Leek, is a preserved flint grinding mill. The picturesque site is adjacent to the Caldon Canal and a preserved narrow boat is moored here. Flint stones were

One of the two waterwheels at the Cheddleton Flint Mill

calcined in kilns and ground to powder and then used in the Potteries to make bone china, hence its local importance. There are two water-wheels and the mill has become an important tourist attraction, where the whole process is demonstrated and the machinery can be seen in motion.

Although one can no longer travel by British Rail in this immediate vicinity, two steam railway centres have been established. At Ched-dleton, the old railway station about a mile downstream from the mill can be visited. It has a small collection of steam locomotives and rolling stock and a museum devoted to the North Staffordshire Railway. Currently there is a proposal to turn the disused Churnet Valley Railway into a tourist line. A little further south at the Foxfield Light Railway near to Dilhorne, just off the Cheadle to Stoke-on-Trent road, you can take a ride on a steam train for a few miles along a restored colliery line.

It has already been indicated that there are many beauty spots in the Churnet Valley but quite a few do demand that you leave the car behind. Furthermore the lack of roads down the valley, a feature particularly pertinent in the Dane as well as the Churnet, does mean exploring both sides separately.

The Caldon Canal at Consall Forge

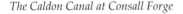

The main appeal of the Churnet lies below Cheddleton, where the valley bottom can be followed along the canal towpath to Froghall and rewards the effort. If you are particularly interested in canals and their architecture, take your car to **Denford**, just off the Leek to Hanley road (A53) at Longsdon. Walk westwards past the canalside pub (The Hollybush) under the aqueduct which carries the Leek arm of the canal, to Hazelhurst locks, where the Froghall branch locks down. There is a canal keeper's cottage, a rather nice cast-iron footbridge and much to interest the photographer.

The Cheddleton to Froghall section really starts at Basford Bridge near the railway station. The valley is well wooded and the leafy glades provide a marvellous backcloth for the canal. **Consall Forge** is a small hamlet on the canal. Steep steps descend from each side of the valley to reach it, giving a more direct access than along the canal towpath. The hamlet gets its name from an old iron forge which existed in Elizabethan times, but all trace of it has long gone. Here, the canal and river run in one channel — a broad expanse of slow moving water which separates again in front of the old canal pub — the Black Lion, now the preserve of ramblers and pleasure boat users. The canal disappears under a footbridge and the railway to meander casually down to Froghall and the wharf there. The river commences its own course once more at the foot of a large weir and the whole scene is worth stopping to examine and photograph. Look out also for the remains of the huge lime kilns near to the canal. There ia a Nature Centre situated on the road between Consall and Consall Forge.

Below Consall Forge is the former Podmore's Flint Mill, the last surviving local flint crushing mill serving the pottery industry. It was still using water power — but turbines and not waterwheels, which had been removed — until recently. Two to three miles further on is **Froghall** with its vast copper works and canal wharf. Here a picnic area has been created at the canal basin, and one can explore the old limekilns and loading docks where limestone was loaded onto railway wagons or into narrow boats. The quarry wagons ran on a 3ft 6in gauge track and lengths of rail of this gauge remain. With the 2ft 6in gauge of the Manifold Valley Light Railway, the North Staffordshire Railway was the only railway company in Britain to have lines of three different gauges. The incline to the quarry at **Cauldon Low** was the second oldest in the country, dating from 1777. If you are in Froghall with a car, take the Kingsley road and take the first turn right along a narrow lane which gives several views down into the valley and is particularly useful if time does not permit a walk. It eventually passes a footpath marked 'Consull' [sic]. A quarter of a mile walk down here gives further excellent views into the valley and access to the canal towpath at Podmore's Flint Mill.

The valley between Froghall and **Oakamoor** is denied even to the rambler but the latter village is worth investigation. It has two old pubs and a picnic site on the foundations of an old copper works, demolished in 1963 and now consolidated at Froghall. Here Messrs Thomas Bolton & Sons manufactured the copper wire core for the first transatlantic cable in 1856. Other than a few date stones, nothing now remains of the works except for a very large mill pool, the retained water cascading down a stepped weir before disappearing under the road bridge. Within a short walking distance is Cotton Dell, which is well wooded and quite attractive. A path leaves the B5417 at SK057450 and crosses the dell, which is private. It leaves Star Wood to rejoin the Whiston road above Oakamoor.

The section of valley between Oakamoor and Alton offers a choice of routes. The road via Farley leaves the valley, affording views of the latter and the Weaver Hills. It goes through **Farley** village with its attractive cottages and beautiful hall, once the home of the Bill family. Beyond Farley, the views are towards Alton Towers, its turrets soaring above the trees. The more direct route to Alton keeps to the valley bottom. The road is narrow but rewards patience in summer months. On reaching the former Pink Lodge, now a café and restaurant, walk westwards up Dimmingsdale to the former mill and its beautiful pools beyond. **Alton** village once enjoyed the patronage of the Earls of Shrewsbury who owned almost everything in the area. Look out for the village lock-up and the castle. The valley bottom at Alton has much to offer. The view up to the castle, perched high on the rocks above, looks like a Rhineland replica. The old railway station, built by A. W. N. Pugin, has been restored, while opposite is an old watermill. It is difficult to imagine that this old mill was once a copper and brass wire mill, producing 'Guinea-rods' in huge quantities as currency for the African slave trade. Look out for the lodge to the Towers, also attributed to Pugin.

An important tourist attraction in this south-western region is the former home of the Earls of Shrewsbury, **Alton Towers**. This huge mansion is situated near to Alton village in the Churnet Valley. Today the great house is a gutted shell, but the grounds have been developed as a leisure park, with many attractions for young and old, including its famous 'Corkscrew' which loops twice. Over the last few years, the grounds have been developed into a massive leisure park on the Disneyland theme. The gardens were once billed

WALKS IN THE CHURNET VALLEY

There are a variety of walks which enable the valley to be seen at its best, particularly as the beauty spots are, for the most part, denied to the motorist. The canal towpath from Froghall, where there is a picnic site, can be used to gain access to Consall Forge. Alternatively there are two paths which descend more directly to the hamlet. The towpath from Froghall, as distinct from Cheddleton which can be muddy, is useful for pushing wheelchairs, although there is a bridge with steps to cross.

The more direct paths descend to the Churnet from Consall village and from Belmont. In each case there are numerous steps to descend but Consall Forge is well worth the effort. Park in Consall village and walk eastwards towards the valley. At a bend in the road, a signpost to Consall Forge indicates the start of a well used path which crosses fields before descending down into the valley (1½ miles).

The more interesting route to the river is from Belmont pools, down the 'Devil's Staircase'. The 200 steps descend from the wood near Belmont pools through the estate of Belmont Hall (not open to the public). Park at Belmont pools on the Cheddleton to

Ipstones road and the path (not the hall drive) taken to Consall Forge. The pools are popular with photographers — the huge beech trees create a perfect setting for the artificial pools. By the road here is an old chapel with its small tower and east window. It did not have a religious use for long and was built when the owner of the hall fell out with the vicar of Ipstones. It has been carefully restored but like the hall it is a private residence and is not open to the public.

The gardens at Alton Towers

as the largest domestic gardens in Europe. Now Alton Towers is billed as Europe's premier leisure park with over 120 rides, shows and other attractions, including the world's largest log flume (2,600ft in length), a circus and two cineramas. The contrasts seem endless: rides for small children and rides that look terrifying; the delightfully situated licensed restaurant in the Swiss Cottage overlooking the garden and the Talbot Restaurant, the largest fast-food restaurant in Europe; peace and quiet in the gardens and ruins of the house while just the opposite are the theme areas of Fantasy World, Festival Park, Talbot Street, Aqualand, Towers Street, Kiddies Kingdom etc.

Of particular interest are the gardens, where hundreds of workmen toiled to convert a whole valley into a magnificent garden. It gained its effect by 'impressiveness of sheer profusion' as one writer put it. Around the valley are many paths and steps and one can find a corkscrew fountain, a Gothic temple, a three storey 'Stonehenge', a Swiss chalet, a huge range of conservatories and much use of water. In the summer one can often hear a band playing in the bandstand and over the tree tops, see water shooting into the sky from a 'Chinese Pagoda' fountain, its gold painted bells glistening through the falling water. There is much to see here and although at first glance it appears not to be cheap to gain admittance for the family, it is well worth going for a whole day. Alton Towers is a big place attracting big crowds so go early in the morning. You may prefer to make your visit mid-week when there are sometimes less people about and less queuing for attractions especially in the spring or autumn. The gardens are particularly worth seeing in the May when the rhododendrons are in flower. At this time of year you can appreciate what 'impressiveness of sheer profusion' really means.

The Dane and Upper Goyt Valleys

The Dane Valley, with its tributary the Clough Brook, rivals the Churnet and Dove Valleys as a major beauty spot in the west of the Peak District. Rising on Whetstone Edge, close to the Cat and Fiddle Inn, its deeply cut valley confines the infant waters of the river. Using old packhorse routes as paths it is possible to walk down much of the valley. The old bridge at **Three Shires Head** should not be missed. Have a look underneath it to see that the bridge has been widened at some time either for increased horse traffic or for the passage of carts.

A couple of miles downstream from the bridge is **Gradbach**, a scattered community with no village as such. It is easily approached off the A53, the Leek to Buxton road, through **Flash**, the highest village in England. This is a harsh village of weather worn cottages, huddled together on the side of Oliver Hill. Descending down to the Dane, the scenery is more interesting and the climate more tolerant. Gradbach is worth taking time to explore. Not having a village centre, it is best to park at the car park on the lane to the youth hostel and by the side of the river. Look for the old Methodist Chapel, built in 1849, and the adjacent cottage by the bridge over the river before walking downstream towards Gradbach Mill and Back Forest. It is easy to find, simply take the road to Flash from the bridge and turn first right down the side of a small brook. It is however a narrow road and it is better to walk than take the car once the car park is reached.

Gradbach Mill is now owned by the Youth Hostels Association, but used to be a silk mill with a large waterwheel fed by water from the Dane. It was rebuilt in 1758 following a fire, and closed down as a silk mill about 100 years later. Its large waterwheel was scrapped in the 1950s. A good example of an old packhorse road can be seen ascending the hill on the opposite side of the river from the mill. Below the mill lies Lud Church and Back Forest which was stripped of its main timber in the mid 1950s. **Lud Church** has already been mentioned but it is worth repeating that it repays a visit, preferably on a walk from Gradbach by way of Hanging Stone to Danebridge and Swythamley (8 miles). Much of the area south of the river between Gradbach and Danebridge formed part of the Swythamley Estate which was divided and sold in 1977. The estate also included Swythamley Hall, plus the Roaches. The latter were purchased in 1980 by the National Park in a deal costing £185,000.

If the walk mentioned above is taken, stop near the Hanging Stone. The view over Swythamley and south-eastwards towards the Roaches is worth more than a passing glance. Indeed, before coming over the bluff from Gradbach the view northwards up to the Clough Brook with the high hill of Shutlingsloe rising to 1,659ft is even more interesting. The Hanging Stone carries two plaques, one to a pet dog, the other to the brother of the last Brocklehurst of Swythamley. He was Lieutenant Colonel Brocklehurst, who had been a gamewarden in the Sudan, and who established a private zoo on the Roaches which included deer, a kangaroo, wallabies and a yak. Descendants of the deer still roam these hills. On reaching Danebridge take the well defined path, which starts by the side of the bridge, back to Gradbach through the fields above the River Dane.

Further north under the hill of Shutlingsloe lies **Wildboarclough**. Taking the road westwards from Gradbach, a couple of miles brings one to Allgreave where the minor road joins the A54. Just beyond the

The packhorse bridge over the River Dane at Three Shires Head, where Derbyshire, Staffordshire and Cheshire all meet

Clough Brook a minor road turns off to the right to run northwards towards Shutlingsloe. This road hugs the brook all the way to Wildboarclough. It is an attractive route and passes the Crag Inn, a popular stopping off place for visitors. The village boasted the largest sub post office in England before it closed. This distinction arises from the post office being in what was the administration block of a now demolished textile mill. Traces of the mill can be seen from the road at the T-junction just up river from the Crag Inn. On the hillside above the post office is Crag Hall, the country seat of Lord Derby. The roadway near to the hall abounds with rhododendrons which are a riot of colour in the summer. If time permits, continue upstream for half a mile or so and leave the car where the signpost indicates the path to Cumberland Clough. Walk up the brook past the deep ravine with its rushing white water and dark conifers, to the waterfall before returning to the car (1½ miles).

Just above **Danebridge** the waters of the Clough and Dane unite to form a good sized river flowing beneath the broad arch after which the village takes its name. Like many neighbouring communities, Danebridge consists of a few loosely grouped cottages. It also has an interesting old pub, the Ship Inn, which until recently had some relics of the 1745 uprising, including a flintlock of a Scottish soldier and part of a newspaper he was carrying. The name Ship Inn, is said to be a reminder of the *SS Swithamley* [*sic*], although the present inn

Gradbach Silk Mill, now a youth hostel

sign is of the *Nimrod* which took Shackleton, and Sir Phillip Brockle-hurst of Swythamley, to the Antarctic.

The broad fields below Danebridge, broken by areas of woodland and views of Bosley Cloud, make a pleasant walk to Gig Hall Bridge where the feeder channel to Rudyard reservoir starts. Above the valley is Wincle Grange Farm where the monks of old had a sheep and cattle farm. Further north, and connected by a track to the grange is Cleulow Cross, now hidden by the trees which surround it. It was probably a waymark cross on the route to the coast from Dieulacresse Abbey at Leek, which had important holdings of sheep and is known to have exported wool to Italy.

From Gig Hall Bridge, the feeder supply winds down the valley to **Rushton**. It has a path at the side, much in the nature of a towpath, which provides a pleasant walk. Below the village lies Rudyard Lake, built by John Rennie as a water supply to the Trent and Mersey Canal and today a popular resort for yachtsmen and fishermen.

North of the Dane lies **Macclesfield Forest**, the high moorland of Shining Tor and the Goyt. The road upstream from Wildboarclough can be used as a good introduction to the area. Turn first left (above the village, opposite Dryknowle Farm). The road soon enters the forest to pass between Trentabank and Ridgegate Reservoirs. Upon reaching Trentabank Reservoir, there is a visitor centre, car park and toilets. There are woodland trails here plus a large heronry. Upon reaching the road junction opposite the pub turn right up the narrow road which climbs steeply uphill. A deviation to the left and into Tegg's Nose Country Park may be made if time permits. The narrow road climbs up to the hamlet of Macclesfield Forest with its little, rugged chapel and school. Continue to Bottom-of-the-Oven and then drive up the lane northwards to Lamaload Reservoir. It has a picnic area at its northern end which is a quieter stopping place than at Errwood Reservoir, in the Goyt Valley.

From Lamaload, proceed to Jenkin Chapel erected in 1733 at John Slack's expense as a tablet records. Turn eastwards and climb over Pym Chair before dropping down to the twin reservoirs of Errwood and Fernilee.The former rivals Rudyard Lake with its yachts and there is a picnic site overlooking the water. The ruins of Errwood Hall near the south-western end of the water are an interesting detour, particularly when the rhododendrons are in bloom. Leave the Goyt after crossing the dam. The steep inclined road was formerly part of the Cromford and High Peak Railway and wagons used to be hauled up the incline by a steam engine at the top. The reservoir at the top of the incline provided water for the engine's boiler.

WALKS IN THE DANE VALLEY

The area around Three Shires Head has several old packhorse routes which can be used for exploration. The one from Flash Bar (ie The Travellers Rest pub at SK 032679) via Drystone Edge and Blackclough can be used for wheelchairs, if you do not mind the path being a little rough in places. It has a tarmac or stone surface for much of its way but is not open to motor vehicles. You may return by Turn Edge to make a 5 mile circular route although this is not recommended for wheelchairs. Further down the Dane, the path from Danebridge to Gradbach, to include Lud Church, is worth considering (see above) together with the path downstream from Danebridge at least as far as the start of the feeder supply to Rudyard Lake, at Gig Hall Bridge (3 miles).

A recommended 9 mile circular route, takes in the Dane and Clough Brook. For convenience, start at Wildboarclough where there is adequate roadside car parking. Just upstream of the Crag Inn take the footbridge over the brook and climb over the hill to the main road (A54) and Tagsclough Hill. From here, this old packhorse route continues straight to Gradbach Mill via Burntcliff Top. It emerges at the Flash to Allgreave road by the side of an old pub, the Eagle and Child, now a private house. Inside the entrance is a plaque depicting an eagle and child taken from the arms of the Stanleys, Earls of Derby, who own Crag Hall and its estate at Wildboarclough. From Gradbach Mill proceed upstream to the chapel where a path cuts up the hill, east of the Dane to Turn Hill where it meets the packhorse route to Three Shires Head from Flash. Cross the bridge at Three Shires Head and continue over to Cumberland Clough via Holt Farm and the western edge of Dane Bower. Follow the clough down to the road and turn downstream to Wildboarclough.

North of the Dane, the upper Goyt down to Errwood Reservoir makes a good 3 mile walk, together with some time spent exploring the ruins of Errwood Hall and its grounds. Cars must be parked at Derbyshire Bridge, or at the car park on the hillside above the dam, but on Sundays in summer a minibus is available to take you much nearer to Errwood. If you visit the area midweek and drive from the Pym Chair, or west side of the valley, you can drive down to Errwood and out via Derbyshire Bridge.

There are youth hostels at Dimmings Dale near to Oakamoor for the Churnet Valley and at Meerbrook. The hostel at Gradbach enables the Dane Valley to be explored easily.

*Crag Hall and
Shutlingsloe*

*Goyt Bridge upstream
from Errwood
Reservoir*

*Gawsworth Hall,
south of Macclesfield*

Lyme Hall

Macclesfield is an old textile town which initially expanded with the building of the Macclesfield Canal and later the railway. Of particular interest to visitors are the Silk Mill and Heritage Centre — the only museum in Britain devoted to the silk industry. It is housed in the former Sunday School and includes a restored Victorian classroom. Nearby Paradise Mill may dispute the Silk Mill and Heritage Centre's claim to fame for it is a working museum of the town's former silk industry. Twenty-six hand-powered Jacquard looms survive and practical demonstrations are given.

Between Macclesfield and Macclesfield Forest is the Tegg's Nose Country Park, based around an old sandstone quarry. A static exhibit about the quarry uses some of the original equipment, and there are various walks which start from the carpark. Another walk is the Middlewood Way, a reclaimed railway line 11 miles long between Macclesfield and Middlewood, which is useful for cycling and horse riding, or it can be used as part of a circular path incorporating the Macclesfield Canal or the Gritstone Trail.

The Gritstone Trail is a 20 mile path from Lyme Park, near Disley to Rushton near Leek. It links with the Staffordshire Way to make a long distance path and passes through Tegg's Nose Country Park. A leaflet about the trail is available from nearby tourist information centres. Both these trails have memorable views in almost all directions.

The Macclesfield area has several country houses open to the public. Adlington Hall to the north dates mainly from the fifteenth century with a Regency south front. It is a beautiful half-timbered house set in fine grounds. The great hall is a particulary interesting survival, while the Georgian barn is now a tea room.

West of Macclesfield is Capesthorne Hall, with a massive front longer than Buckingham Palace. Its central portion was rebuilt by Salvin after a disastrous fire in the nineteenth century. South of the town is Gawsworth Hall, a serene place which dates from 1480, although part was demolished in 1701 when the house was remodelled.

At the northern extremity of this area, and right on the edge of the conurbation south of Manchester, is Lyme Hall on the A6 near Disley, 6½ miles south of Stockport. It was built in Elizabethan times and enlarged in the eighteenth and nineteenth centuries. This large house, now owned by the National Trust, has a Palladian south front reminiscent of Chatsworth's west front, gardens and a large deer park. Inside there is fine furniture and one of the most important collections of early English clocks outside London.

Additional Information

Places to Visit

Churnet Valley

Alton Towers Leisure Park
Alton, 3 miles east of Cheadle
☎ (0538) 702200
Open: major rides and attractions:
mid-March to early November
daily 10am-5, 6 or 7pm depending
on season. Grounds and gardens:
all year round 9am-1 hour after
attractions close, with much
reduced admission rate in winter.
Over 120 rides and attractions, free
once entrance fee has been paid.
Theme areas and magnificent
gardens, on former estate of the
Earls of Shrewsbury. Over fifty
catering outlets, free parking,
facilities for the disabled.

Leek

Brindley Water Mill
Mill Street
☎ Leek (0538) 381000
Open: Easter-October, weekends and
Bank Holiday Mondays, 2-5pm; July
and August, also Monday, Tuesday
and Wednesday 2-5pm.
Operational cornmill. Museum of
the life and times of James
Brindley, engineer, 1716-72.

Coombes Valley Nature Reserve
Six Oaks Farm, nr Apesford
Open: Tuesday, Thursday and
weekends.

Deep Hayes Country Park
Wallgrange, on the road to
Cheddleton from Longsdon, south-
west of Leek.
Waymarked nature trail and
information centre.
Visitor Centre open: May-Septem-
ber, Saturday and Sunday, 2-5pm.

North Staffordshire Railway Centre
Cheddleton Station, Cheddleton
3 miles from Leek, off A520 to Stone
☎ (0538) 360522 (Sundays);
(0782) 503458 (other times)
Open: Easter to September,
Sundays and Bank Holiday
Mondays 11am-5.30pm. At other
times by prior arrangement.
Ornate Victorian station building
housing café, souvenir shop and
small relics museum. Also signal
box, locomotive display hall. Steam
rides on most open days.

Macclesfield

Bollington Discovery Centre
Grimshaw Lane,
Bollington
☎ (0625) 572681
Open: Easter-Christmas Monday-
Friday 2-4.30pm, Saturday &
Sunday 10am-4.30pm.
Visitor centre alongside Maccles-
field Canal and Middlewood Way.
Cycle and canoe hire.

Capesthorne Hall
Siddington
☎ Chelford (0625) 861221
Caravans & camping (0625) 861779
Open: April, Sunday only; May,
August & September, Wednesday
& Sunday; June & July, Tuesday-
Thursday & Sunday. Open Good
Friday and all Bank Holidays.
Park, gardens and chapel 12noon-
6pm; hall 2.30-4.30pm.
House dates from 1719 with
substantial nineteenth-century
alterations. Georgian chapel, Mill
Wood Walk, gardens with nature
trail, park and lakes. 100 pitches for
touring caravans/tents.

Gawsworth Hall
Gawsworth, 2½ miles south of
Macclesfield on the A536
☎ North Rode (0260) 223456
Open: April-October, daily 2-5.30pm.
Striking fifteenth-century half-
timbered hall with beautiful
gardens. Open-air theatre with
covered grandstand, mid-June to
August.

Macclesfield Silk Museum
Heritage Centre,
Roe Street
☎ (0625) 613210 for information
Open: Tuesday-Saturday 11am-
5pm, Sunday 2-5pm. Closed
Mondays (except Bank Holidays),
New Year's Day, Good Friday,
Christmas Day and Boxing Day.
Admission fee charged.
First museum in Britain to be
devoted entirely to the study of the
silk industry. Award winning
audio-visual programme. Costume,
textiles, room settings, scale
models. Museum shop. Tea room.

Paradise Silk Mill
Park Lane
☎ (0625) 618228 for information
Open: Tuesday-Sunday 2-5pm.
Closed Mondays (except Bank
Holidays), New Year's Day, Good
Friday, Christmas Day and Boxing
Day. Admission fees charged.
Guides demonstrate weaving and
work the ancillary machinery for
visitors. Jacquard handlooms in
their original setting restored to
demonstrate the skills of a dying
craft. Exhibitions and room
settings. Museum shop.

West Park Museum
Prestbury Road
☎ (0625) 619831 for information

Open: Tuesday-Sunday 2-5pm.
Closed Mondays (except Bank
Holidays), 1 Jan, Good Friday,
Christmas Day and Boxing Day.
Wide range of fine and decorative
art material and objects relating to
local history. Also a small but
significant collection of Egyptian
antiquities. The museum is a venue
for a variety of touring exhibitions.

Stockport
Lyme Hall and Park
(National Trust)
Disley, 6 miles from Stockport
☎ Disley (0663) 762023
Open: Hall, summer months, check
specific dates; Park all year round.
1,300 acre park with red and fallow
deer. 17 acres of historic gardens.
Hall with guides in Edwardian
servant's costumes. Many treasures
including a large clock collection.

Craft Centres

Old Shop Craft Pottery
High Street, Alton, Staffs
☎ Oakamoor (0538) 702065
Open: every afternoon and Monday,
Tuesday and Wednesday mornings.
Decorated earthenware, stoneware,
sculpture.

Tourist Information Offices

Congleton
Town Hall, High Street
☎ Congleton (0260) 271095

Leek
Market Place
☎ Leek (0538) 381000

Macclesfield
Town Hall, Market Place.
☎ Macclesfield (0625) 504114

2
DOVEDALE &
THE MANIFOLD VALLEY

Both the Rivers Dove and Manifold rise on the grits and shales of Axe Edge, in close proximity to each other and to the Rivers Goyt, Dane and Wye which divide this bleak upland area into different watersheds. All these rivers flow down deeply incised courses contrasting with the shallow valley of the River Hamps, the main tributary of the Manifold. The infant Dove and Manifold both rise close to the Traveller's Rest Inn at Flash Bar some 7½ miles up the Buxton road out of Leek. The River Dove forms the county boundary between Derbyshire and Staffordshire and its source is in a small well close to the road, marked with intertwined initials of CC and IW — Charles Cotton and Izaak Walton. This is a replica of the monogram carved on the fishing house in Beresford Dale downstream, but was erected in 1851, two centuries after both men fished the waters of the river. The Manifold's source can also be seen from the road, just to the south of the inn. Starting in a shallow depression, it is deeply cut into the landscape before leaving the field in which it rises.

The upper reaches of both rivers are quite spectacular and can be viewed easily by taking the Hollinsclough road from the Traveller's Rest Inn. The road soon climbs Edge Top where one can pull off the road and view both valleys at the same time. At this point the Manifold has cut deeply into the gritstone formations but the more spectacular view is towards Hollinsclough and the hills beyond. It is here that the overlying grits are replaced by the older limestones. These are chiefly bedded but characteristic of this side of the limestone and gritstone boundary are the reef knolls which are in massive limestone, and have not yet yielded in the same way to the forces of erosion. The result is a succession of hills on the edge of the limestone plateau which stretch down the Dove and to a much lesser extent occur in the Manifold as well. Examples are Hollins Hill, Chrome Hill, Parkhouse Hill, High Wheeldon, Thorpe Cloud, and Thor's Cliff; they are the closest one gets to 'peaks' in the Peak District. The fossil content of these rocks is also much more varied: while the bedded rocks contain chiefly crinoids and brachiopods, sea lilies (which are animals and not plants) and bivalve shells, the reefs also contain a greater variety of fossils such as trilobites, corals and goniatites. However, try to obtain samples from quarry spoil heaps; do not hammer indiscriminately and without permission.

Beyond Hollinsclough, the character of the two valleys changes. The Dove flows through a deep limestone valley past Crowdecote towards Hartington, while the Manifold, still flowing across the softer overlying shales, occupies a very broad and shallow valley. This difference can easily be seen by taking the Longnor to Sheen road, which runs along the rounded bluff between both rivers which are less than a mile apart at one point.

Below Hartington and Hulme End both rivers occupy gorge-like valleys cut deeply into the limestone. The broad valley of the Manifold suddenly ends at the huge limestone dome of Ecton Hill. Hereafter it is characterised by huge incised meanders that wind in an interlocking pattern down to Ilam where the two rivers unite. It is these spectacular meanders which give the river its name. This creates an ever-changing subject for the eye and camera and as a result the scenery is more varied than the Dove Valley and also more interesting until one reaches the Milldale to Thorpe Cloud section of the River Dove. This is Dovedale — a majestic stretch of the valley now unfortunately suffering from over-use by ramblers. With its natural ashwoods, numerous towers of natural stone and features such as Pickering Tor, The Twelve Apostles, Reynard's Arch and the Watchbox near Ilam Rock, it has much to commend it. Much of Dovedale is protected by the National Trust and the dale forms the major part of the Trust's South Peak Estate. It is also a Site of Special Scientific Interest: Grade 1, because of its relict ash wood. While many people stop at Ilam Rock few glance down river to try and spot the Watchbox, a huge mass of stone perched high on the cliffs of the Derbyshire bank. It is supposed to be capable of being rocked by hand, but the author has never tried to prove whether this is true.

Between Ilam and Thorpe the two rivers unite. The Manifold is by far the larger river, but as the Dove is the county boundary it carries its name downstream from here until it reaches the River Trent near Burton. One of the main tributaries of these two rivers is the Hamps which flows off Morridge near to Leek, in a very broad valley to

Waterhouses where it too reaches the limestone and enters a deeply incised valley like the Manifold. It twists and turns with almost monotonous regularity until it joins the Manifold beneath the huge cliffs of Beeston Tor, which was purchased by the National Trust in 1976. An unusual feature of both the Hamps and the Manifold is the disappearance of the water during dry spells. The Hamps is swallowed up at Waterhouses down solution cavities in the limestone known as 'swallets' or elsewhere in the Peak as 'shack-holes'. There are more swallets at Wetton Mill on the Manifold (on private ground) and a second group can be seen from the road just below Wetton Mill at Redhurst, just before the Wetton road begins to climb out of the valley. Both rivers occupy different underground channels and do not appear to unite. Coloured dyes take some 22-24 hours to re-emerge at the boilholes in the grounds of Ilam Hall, close to the riverside path.

Clearly the deep valleys have had an influence on the distribution and location of the many small villages scattered throughout the area. The upper and less productive soils have resulted in scattered farmhouses rather than communities and Longnor is the only village of any size, growing at the junction of two turnpike roads in the eighteenth century. Elsewhere the villages are situated on the rolling plateau above the valleys, with the notable exceptions of Hartington and Ilam. Waterhouses assumed some importance with the coming of the Manifold Valley Light Railway in 1904 although the railhead at Hulme End failed to develop, primarily because of the economic unimportance of its existence. The only towns of any size are outside the area at Buxton, Leek (described in other chapters) and Ashbourne, each exerting some influence over parts of the area, particularly Leek and Ashbourne which have cattle markets.

Settlement in the area can be traced back to the Palaeolithic or Old Stone Age period. Many of the caves in the valleys have yielded evidence of early occupation, chiefly for shelter, although some such as Ossum's Cave at Wetton Mill are known to have been occupied as a workshop for fashioning flints. Even the large Thor's Cave was occupied at one stage. Many of the finds of these caves can be viewed in Buxton Museum, while other finds from Thor's Cave now form part of the Bateman Collection in Sheffield Museum.

Many burials were made in the numerous 'lows' or tumuli which are scattered across the area, but chiefly east of the River Manifold. Excavation of these was undertaken by Thomas Bateman, a nineteenth-century barrow-digger. Victorian antiquarians are usually frowned upon as their techniques were often crude and the results

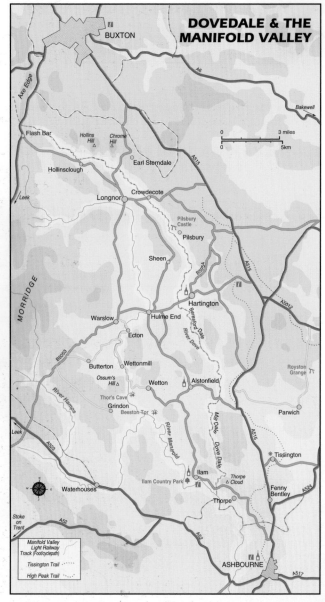

DOVEDALE & THE MANIFOLD VALLEY

BUXTON

Bakewell

Axe Edge

Flash Bar

Hollins Hill △

Chrome Hill △

Earl Sterndale

Hollinsclough

Leek

Longnor

Crowdecote

Pilsbury Castle

Pilsbury

Sheen

Hartington

MORRIDGE

Warslow

Hulme End

Ecton

Butterton

Wettonmill

Ossum's Hill △

Wetton

Alstonfield

Royston Grange

River Hamps

Thor's Cave

Grindon

Beeston Tor

Parwich

Leek

River Manifold

Beresford Dale

River Dove

Mill Dale

Dove Dale

Tissington

Waterhouses

Ilam Country Park

Ilam

Thorpe Cloud

Fenny Bentley

Thorpe

Stoke on Trent

ASHBOURNE

0   3 miles
0   5km

Manifold Valley
Light Railway
Track (Foot/cyclepath)

Tissington Trail ....

High Peak Trail -·-·-·-

Thorpe Cloud (right) and the entrance to Dovedale

Hollinsclough in Upper Dovedale

poorly documented. Bateman was somewhat better than most of his contemporaries, although he did open four burial mounds (at Hurdlow, close to the Earl Sterndale to Brierlow Bar road) in one day!

Nearby in Dowel Dale is a cave situated close to the road and just above Dowall Hall Farm. Excavation of this cave yielded a communal burial of late Neolithic (or New Stone Age) date. There were skeletons of ten people, ranging from a baby to an old man, interred in the cave. Excavations by the Peakland Archaeological Society at Fox Hole Cave on High Wheeldon have yielded remains dating back to the Middle Stone Age.

The Bronze Age and Iron Age are represented in the area through cave and tumuli excavation. There are none of the hillforts in the area which characterise other parts of the Peak. The Bronze Age people used caves for shelter but buried their dead in barrows or mounds of earth which were raised over a grave or a cremation. A good example of a barrow can be seen adjacent to the road at the Liffs on the Hartington to Alsop road, east of Biggin Dale, just into the field at the top of the hill. Liffs Low contained a cist made of slabs of limestone and contained two sets of flint axes, flint spearheads, flint knives and flint arrow heads among other material.

The more recent history of the area shows little Roman influence, although the area was occupied and farmed by Romano-British settlers at the time. A Roman coin of Severius was found at Hulme End during excavations for a cottage but no Roman encampments were established in the area. A motte and bailey castle was established north of Hartington at Pilsbury in Norman times, but little is known about it and full details await excavation. There is, however, a useful interpretation board, which enables the layout of this complex site, alongside a public footpath up the valley, to be better appreciated.

The caves of the Manifold have also yielded a further find of much interest. During excavation of St Bertram's Cave at Beeston Tor in 1924, forty-nine Anglo-Saxon silver pennies of about AD871-4 were recovered. In addition there were two silver brooches and three gold rings. All are now preserved in the British Museum.

In the Middle Ages parts of the area became the property of various religious orders and a small level platform at Musden Grange near Ilam is the supposed remains of the monastic grange. Following the dissolution of the monasteries the lands passed into private ownership and thereafter much land was under the influence of such families as the Duke of Devonshire — particularly at Hartington, Ecton and Wetton. The oldest son of the Duke of Devonshire is in fact Lord Hartington. Other estates were those of the Harpur Crewes (who owned much land around Warslow, Longnor and Alstonfield) and the FitzHerberts at Tissington.

Historical and literary associations with the area are numerous — particularly as a result of the popularity of Dovedale. Byron and Dr Johnson for example were visitors to the dale; Jean Jacques Rousseau knew it during his exile at nearby Wootton Hall; William Morris and other pre-Raphaelites, as well as Mark Twain, were visitors to Sir Thomas Wardle at Swainsley in the Manifold Valley. Perhaps the greatest name associated with the Dove is that of Izaak Walton who used to stay with his close friend — who became his adopted son — Charles Cotton. Cotton owned Beresford Hall and the Dove flowed through his estate. Beresford Dale is one of the prettiest places on the whole of the river although Dutch Elm disease has killed many trees and their removal has marred the dale. It was here that Cotton built a fishing house, dated 1674, which still survives. Cotton added chapters to Walton's *Compleat Angler* in the fifth edition before Walton died, his fame assured. Cotton also owned Throwley Hall at one time, but both Beresford and Throwley Halls are no more. Only a prospect tower survives at Beresford, but the ruins of Throwley can be seen from the Calton to Ilam road. The fishing house is on private land, but can be seen from the footpath as one approaches the trees at the north end of the dale from Hartington.

In the past, people of the area found work chiefly in agriculture and to a lesser extent in the extractive industries or small waterpowered mills. It is a pattern reflected in all parts of the Peak. There is not a great deal to see of these former activities although early enclosures around Calton and south-east of Longnor preserve the ancient strip pattern of cultivation in the narrow fields that survive. The insular nature of former village communities seems to be reflected at Butterton where the field walls are built almost as circles around the village. Narrow cultivation terraces — or lynchets — can be found quite frequently in the lower parts of the valleys. A particularly fine set can be seen near Throwley Hall from the opposite side of the valley (ie south of Wetton), particularly when the sun is low in the sky. They are situated in the shallow valley between Throwley and Beeston Tor. The early strip field system is preserved well in the fields to the west of the Buxton-Ashbourne road, between the turnings to Tissington.

Much of the stone for dry stone walls was quarried locally and many small quarries and lime kilns can be found. There are several, for instance, in Hartington Dale between the village and its old railway station. It was quite common for a farmer to have his own lime kiln to burn stone for his land. A good quality gritstone was even mined at Daisy Knoll Farm, Longnor, providing much of the building stone for the village.

There are also many mines in the area. In the millstone grit of Axe Edge, coal was mined, while lower downstream lead, copper and zinc ores were extracted, which yielded varying fortunes or losses for the miners. At Ecton near Warslow, various mines, which yielded considerable quantities of copper ore can be observed from the roads or footpaths. The main mine reached a total depth of over 1,400ft — the deepest mine in Britain in the eighteenth century — and made a

Thor's Cave in the Manifold Valley, once inhabited by prehistoric man

The bridge over the River Manifold at Wetton Mill

The old market hall at Longnor. The village is a popular base for exploring the upper reaches of both the Manifold and Dove Valleys

considerable fortune for the Duke of Devonshire, its owner. It had an early example of a Boulton and Watt steam engine, an underground canal for haulage purposes and several other unusual features, including a waterwheel for pumping, situated deep underground.

The waters of the main streams have long been used for water power. There were medieval mills at Hartington, Ilam and Okeover for instance. The cornmill at Lode Mill near Alstonfield remains intact, while Brund Mill west of Sheen and Hartington Mill have been converted to delightful dwellinghouses. Longnor's sawmill is also slowly being rebuilt as a house. Some of the water mills have had a varied history. Brund Mill was built in 1760 as a cornmill, but in 1790 this fine building was converted into a cotton mill by Thomas Cantrell, who got into financial difficulties with it four years later. It ended its days grinding corn during World War II and slowly fell into disrepair before being tastefully converted to a dwelling and retaining much of the machinery. Thomas Cantrell also had a cotton mill in Hartington which was built about 1776 on the site of what is now Minton House. The little cottages opposite were probably for his workers; they bear the initial T & JC 1777.

Little industry has survived to the present day. Two notable exceptions are the Hartington Stilton Cheese Factory and the silica fire-brick works at Friden — both remnants of long established industries. Cheese was formerly made at Glutton Bridge north of Longnor and Derby cheese was made at Reapsmoor. Both these buildings survive, but the factory established in old mine buildings at Ecton in the 1920s closed in 1933 and all buildings there have been demolished. The Hartington factory, now owned by the Milk Marketing Board, makes Stilton cheese which is exported all around the world. The Friden works commenced extracting sand from local pits in 1892. These are unusual pockets found in the limestone and the deposits are still being worked by DSF Refractories Ltd, making bricks for furnace hearth linings.

Despite being so rural the area was served by three railway lines. The Buxton to Ashbourne line was the most recent, for work commenced as late as 1890. At Parsley Hay it joined the Cromford and High Peak Railway for a while before leaving the latter to enter Buxton. The Cromford and High Peak Railway was built much earlier and is discussed later.

Of more interest perhaps is the narrow gauge (30in) railway that ran down the Manifold Valley from Waterhouses to Hulme End. This railway opened in 1904 and ran for 30 years. The old station buildings (except the coach shed) still remain at Hulme End. It was an unusual railway, with locomotives modelled on those from a narrow gauge line in India.

TOWNS AND VILLAGES

Ashbourne is the main town serving the area. It has much of interest and plenty of things to see. Primarily a market town, it retains many eighteenth-century buildings together with other much older buildings in its main streets, such as the Gingerbread Shop which is timber framed and considered to be fifteenth century. It is probable that the town was originally situated further to the west and nearer the church which is now almost out of the town, but development of a new centre, including the market place, probably began as early as the thirteenth century. Places to look out for in the town include the Green Man and Black's Head Royal Hotel. Its inn sign stretches over the street — it claims to have the longest hotel name in the country — and it has a small courtyard where coaches unloaded. Look at the Black's Head carved on the gallows-style inn sign; on one side he smiles, on the other he is sad. The inn, which is of Georgian origin, has associations with Boswell, who along with Dr Johnson, stayed in the town with a Dr Taylor who owned The Mansion in Church Street.

A walk along the street towards the church is very rewarding. There are many Georgian houses of interest including No 61, The Grey House, which is next to the Old Grammar School. Sir Nikolaus Pevsner described Church Street as one of the finest streets in Derbyshire. The Grammar School was founded in 1585. The central portion with four gables above was the old schoolroom and the schoolmaster's accommodation was at either side, while opposite is The Mansion with the almshouses built in 1614-30 adjacent.

While in the street, visit the church, one of the grandest in the Peak, preferably in early spring when the churchyard is submerged beneath a delightful carpet of daffodils. The oldest part of the existing building dates from the thirteenth century although a Norman crypt has been located. The alabaster monuments in the church are especially notable, as well as a fine carving in marble of Penelope Boothby. There is a church guide book available.

Ashbourne is famed for its Shrovetide football match which occurs on Shrove Tuesday and Ash Wednesday. The ball is thrown up at 2pm in Shaw Croft car park behind the Green Man Inn and the game can continue until 10pm. The ball is made of leather filled with cork. The goals are 3 miles apart, on the site of the old Clifton and Sturston Mills and teams, consisting of hundreds, are known as the 'Up'ards' and 'Down'ards'. The rules are few and the town's shops

Ashbourne is a good base for shopping and exploring the southern part of the Peak District

Ashbourne's church-yard is noted for its springtime daffodils; the Old Grammar School, dating from Elizabethan times, is in the backgound

are boarded up for safety, and even the river is part of the game. It is the object of each team to get the ball back to it's own goal. It is a slow-moving game and it is rare for more than two goals to be scored in a day's play. Ashbourne's game is the last Shrovetide mass football game to be played through the streets and has survived several attempts in the nineteenth century to prevent it.

Ashbourne was also the home of Catherine Booth, the wife of General Booth, the founder of the Salvation Army. There is a plaque to her in Sturston Road almost opposite a garage, and a bust of her in the park. The town is also famous for its gingerbread and has a growing reputation for its high class clothiers. A recent product of the town is Ashbourne Water, which is pumped from the well at the Nestlé factory. It is lightly carbonated before being bottled and marketed. Moorland Publishing also has its home in the town, producing guidebooks which are sold around the world.

Although few of the villages in the area have individual buildings of outstanding architectural merit, many are worth visiting. They are all villages which have enjoyed the patronage of some particular family. What does make them of interest is the variations of vernacular architecture, reflecting changing tastes and different building stones. Working northwards from Ashbourne, the most interesting villages are described briefly below.

Fenny Bentley lies a little way up the A515 Buxton road from Ashbourne. In the church is a curious tomb to Thomas Beresford

St Bertram's Bridge at Ilam

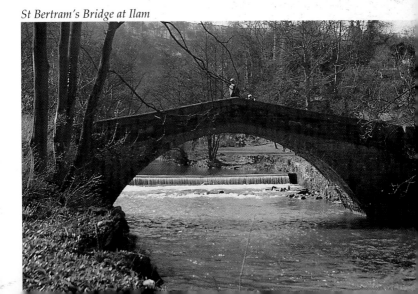

who fought at Agincourt. The effigies of both Thomas and his wife are depicted bundled up in shrouds, as are their twenty-one children around the sides of the tomb. The tower of their fortified and moated manor house may be seen from the A515.

Ilam village was rebuilt away from the Tudor Gothic style hall in the early years of the nineteenth century. The hall was built for Mr Jesse Watts-Russell between 1821 and 1826, to the design of John Shaw, as a spectacular mansion with towers and turrets. This was during the era when Alton Towers was being built in Tudor Gothic style under the influence of Pugin. The author considers that Ilam, built in the same style, was an attempt to 'keep up with the Jones's' — or in this case the Earl of Shrewsbury. Snelston Hall, south of Ashbourne, was similar. All three properties were far too large for domestic comfort, but typical of Victorian affluence. The formal buildings of Ilam Hall were demolished in 1934 and the remaining portion is now a youth hostel, and not open to the public.

The 'model' village, school, hall and church at Ilam are all of interest. There is a National Trust Shop and Information Centre in the old cellar of the hall, while at the rear is a tea-room in the stable block of the Watts-Russell house. The view from the terrace is magnificent and it is easy to see why Ilam Hall was built on this particular site. There are two Saxon crosses in the churchyard and inside the church is the tomb of St Bertram and Sir Francis Chantrey's statue of David Pike-Watts. The latter is very fine indeed and shows Jesse Watts-Russell's father-in-law on his death bed with his daughter and grandchildren at his bedside. The cross in the village near the bridge is dedicated to the daughter, Watts-Russell's wife, Mary. Also worth exploring are the paths in the wood in the grounds of the hall. One leads to a grotto where William Congreve wrote the *Old Bachelor*, and his stone desk and seat are still there. The path along the valley bottom, known as Paradise Walk, takes one past the resurging waters of the Manifold and Hamps. Further on it passes the 'Battle Cross' found when the village was remodelled. A visit to Ilam is a must for any holiday in the Peak.

Tissington is worth a visit at any time, but especially when the well-dressing ceremony takes place. The hall is a large and very fine Jacobean mansion but not open to the public. It is a popular subject for photographers, along with the wells and village pond, while the old railway station site is an access point for the Tissington Trail. A visit to the village on, or just after, Acension Day to see the annual well-dressing ceremony should not be missed. Although well-dressing now takes places in many Peakland villages throughout the

WELL DRESSING

Many Derbyshire villages owe their location to a regular flow of pure water. Springs are especially important on the limestone plateau, where water quickly seeps into cracks in the rock. A regular flow of pure water was of particular importance during periods of drought or pestilence, such as the Black Death. The plague was prevalent in the area from medieval times to the seventeenth century, the village of Curbar being a victim in 1632 and Eyam in 1665-6. Tissington's wells are reputed to have maintained their purity during an outbreak of plague in 1348-9.

Thus the custom of 'dressing' or adorning village wells with flowers may have originated as thanks for the supply of pure water. The custom has been practiced for over 300 years, as a visitor to Staffordshire in 1680 noted that 'They have also a custom in this county … of adorning their wells with boughs and flowers' and that the custom was associated with 'cakes, ale and a little music and dancing'.

Today the wells are decorated with flower petals pressed into clay held in a wooden framework. It is a difficult task that combines hard word work with artistic skill. The clay must be cleaned of impurites before being made into the consistency of plaster. The frames must be soaked (often in the village pond, as at Tissington) to prevent the clay from drying out. The trays often have rows of protruding nails to prevent the damp clay from falling away when the frames are vertical.

The design is sketched onto the wet clay, and then flower petals, berries, moss, lichen, seeds and cones are pressed into the surface. The collecting of the flowers and their application must be all done at the last minute to keep the display looking as fresh as possible. The time of year will determine the types of colour available. and wells that are decorated early, such as Tissington, can have problems with the availability of certain flowers, especially if spring comes late.

The custom is now carried on in many villages in and around the Peak District, throughout the spring and summer. Tissington, with its five wells is the best known; Barlow (northwest of Chesterfield) claims to have dressed wells for the longest unbroken period; while Hartington is one of the most recent to start the tradition. A full list of villages which dress their wells in each month is given in the Fact File.

Well dressing at Tissington. The theme is often biblical, as here at Hands Well with the story of Adam and Eve

Tissington Hall

Hartington Hall, now a youth hostel

Milldale near Alstonfield

RAILWAY TRAILS & CYCLE HIRE

The Peak District has a number of disused railway tracks which have been converted to cycling and walking trails.

When the Leek and Manifold Valley Light Railway closed in 1934, Staffordshire County Council converted it into a footpath, although cycling was banned for several decades. When the Cromford and High Peak Railway, the Ashbourne to Parsley Hay line and the Monsal Dale line were closed, they were similarly converted for leisure use.

These trails are ideal for easy and safe cycling, with cycle hire at most of them (see the Fact File for details). Hire is now so popular that it pays to arrive early, or book in advance, especially in the summer and during school holidays. On sunny days and evenings families are often seen straggling out along the old tracks, wending their way admid the flowers and obviously enjoying themselves. Apart from a short section of the Manifold Valley Trail there is no motor traffic, although care must be taken to avoid walkers.

With a little basic map reading it is possible to combine the trails with country lanes to make a circular excursion, to avoid having to return along the same route to a hire centre. Thsi is particulartly so with the Tissington and High Peak Trails, which meet at Parsley Hay. It is possible to gain access to the trail at most road crossings, although a scramble up the embankment may be necessary

Remember that the trails do go uphill, even if with only a slight gradient, especially on the Tissington Trail. The area around Biggin

summer the ceremony at Tissington is the best known. Natural materials, such as flower petals and moss, are pressed into clay set in a wooden frame to form a colourful and unique picture. At Tissington, five wells (plus a children's well) are 'dressed' to depict a particular religious theme. The tradition is supposed to have originated as a thanksgiving for the ceaseless supply of pure water to the village.

Hartington is one of the major tourist centres of the Peak. The hall is dated 1611 and is now a youth hostel. The attractiveness of the village lies in the various houses around the square, which display various forms of vernacular architecture. It is a sobering thought that this individuality of design and construction, all in houses built before planning constraints, seems to be so frowned upon by the planners today, although quite rightly they insist on buildings being

is the highest point and the trail descends northwards and southwards from there. There is also a climb north of Ashbourne up onto the limestone plateau.

The Cromford and High Peak Railway was built like a canal, with long flat sections and inclines between the different levels, so this trail is comparatively level. Both the High Peak and Tissington Trails have reasonable cycling surfaces now (much to the relief of early users of the latter, while the Manifold Valley Trail is surfaced with tarmac.

The Manifold Valley Trail runs from Waterhouses, where there is a hire centre at the old station (access from behind the Crown pub), down the Hamps and Manifold Valleys to Hulme End, near Hartington. If you intend to combine this with the Tissington Trail, remember that the Dove Valley has to be crossed. If you cycle clockwise and do not wish to dismount to ascend from the river, cross at Lode Mill east of Alstonfield, ride down-river to Mill Dale (with a café and toilets) and the cycle up Hope Dale.

On the Tissington Trail there are hire centres at Ashbourne (north of the tunnel) and at Parsley Hay, which also serves the High Peak Trail, which has another hire centre at Middleton Top Engine House near Middleton-by-Wirksworth. The small Sett Valley Trail on the old Hayfield branch line has a hire centre at Hayfield. Another hire centre is at Fairholmes, between Ladybower and Derwent Reservoirs. The Middlewood Way has a hire centre at the Peak and Plains Discovery Centre at Bollington in Cheshire.

built in the local stone. Hartington has several cafés, a hotel, two gift shops and plenty of car parking. It is a good starting point for walks in the area — particularly into Dovedale.

The site of the former Hartington railway station is now a picnic site with toilet facilities, while the railway track has been made into the Tissington Trail. There is an information centre in the old signal box, which still retains its old lever frames and there are several photographs on the wall showing what the railway used to look like. The trail gives level walking and cycling north from Ashbourne. Cycles may be hired from the National Park at Parsley Hay Wharf (SK147636) and Ashbourne (SK175470). If you hire a cycle from Parsley Hay and end up in Hartington, it is better to return via Long Dale, as it is a much easier gradient. Proceed eastwards out of the village, past the school and take the first turn to the left, into Long

Dovedale

Dale. Sections of this valley are part of the Derbyshire Dales National Nature Reserve.

Alstonfield to the south of Hartington is a fine village situated on the limestone plateau, with many solid buildings closely knit together. The church contains many seventeenth-century pews, a double-decker pulpit and a chest about 10ft long and probably 700 years old. Part of the building is Norman and a guide book is available in the church (and also at Hartington Church). In the village, there is a shop and café plus a good pub, the George Inn, well known to ramblers and tourists.

WALKS IN DOVEDALE AND THE MANIFOLD VALLEY

In the dales, there are two places of particular interest which are worth visiting. The whole of the Dove between Hartington and the Stepping Stones near Thorpe is a well known beauty spot and if time does not permit a walk along the river, various roads give access by car. In the Manifold Valley the track-bed of the old railway has been surfaced with tarmac and now provides a useful footpath. A visit to Wettonmill, with its tea-room, and to Thor's Cave a mile or so downstream is essential. If you can find the time the whole track from Waterhouses to Hulme End is well worth walking, although it is a little hard underfoot, and return transport needs to be organised. Even better, hire a bike from the hire centre in the old railway station

Beeston Tor, Manifold Valley

behind the Crown Inn at Waterhouses. It is virtually flat to Hulme End some 8 miles away and easily reached by bike.

There is an abundance of delightful walks in the area. If you wish to walk the dales, there is of course Dovedale itself, between Ilam and Hartington. The dale is, however, being over-used and the tourist authorities no longer wax lyrical about its scenic qualities in order to encourage tourists to visit alternative areas. If you have not seen it, it must be said that it is not to be missed, but try incorporating part of it into a circular walk, which has the advantage of allowing you to get away from the crowds.

Using Ilam as a base, a footpath at the foot of Bunster Hill via the Izaak Walton Hotel leads to the River Dove which can be followed upstream to Ilam Rock. Cross the river here and head up Hall Dale to Stanshope. A path leads from here towards Wetton and upon reaching a narrow lane, the latter should be followed until a path enables you to head for Bincliffe Wood and eventually Castern Hall. This path overlooks the River Manifold and a nature reserve. At Castern, a road is reached which brings one back to Ilam, a total distance of 9 miles.

From Hartington a path leads into the fields by the public toilets, heading for Beresford Dale. On reaching the road at Beresford Dale, where a footbridge and stepping stones cross the river, head for Alstonfield. Depending upon time, this can be either by continuing down Wolfscote Dale and turning uphill after crossing the Dove on a footbridge at Iron Tors, or a more direct route can be taken via Narrowdale. At Alstonfield, head directly to Wetton via Hope Marsh and upon arriving in Wetton take the path northwards between the twin humps of Wetton Hill, returning to Hartington via Back of Ecton and Hulme End. If you do not want to walk up the road from Hulme End to Hartington, head for Beresford Dale and return up river to your car. (Total distance 10 miles.)

The Manifold Valley has a tarmac surfaced path running down from Hulme End and then along the Hamps Valley from Beeston Tor to Waterhouses. Circular routes involving the old railway line are numerous, but of course involve a climb up and out of the valley. Wettonmill is a convenient and a central point from which to start.

A short footpath from Wettonmill proceeding up the Hoo Brook towards Butterton leads to a footbridge. The bridge is on a bridle road from Grindon to Warslow, which runs in an almost straight line between the two villages. A 5 mile circular route can be made by proceeding south towards Grindon. In the last field before reaching the village another path can be taken which heads towards Ladyside

Wood. Enter the wood over a stile by a stone trough and proceed through the wood, slowly terracing around before dropping down into the Manifold Valley close to Thor's Cave. From the valley one can return to Wettonmill by following the former railway track up river. Alternatively cross the river at the footbridge and climb out of the valley heading towards Wetton and return to Wettonmill by the road. This latter alternative gives you superb views of both Thor's Cave and the valley.

A 4½ mile walk starts at the footbridge on the Hoo Brook referred to above (SK087555). Turn northwards up the hill towards Warslow and after crossing the roads from Butterton to Wettonmill and Swainsley respectively, the path drops down to the Warslow Brook before climbing up to Warslow. Just before reaching the B5053 turn to the right and take the path which leads back to Swainsley. Here you can return down the valley to Wettonmill either on the old railway track which is flat, but often busy with traffic in the summer and at weekends, or alternatively by using the old road on the other side of the river. The latter is gated and not used much by traffic.

The whole 8 miles of former railway track between Waterhouses and Hulme End is a useful path for the disabled both with or without wheelchairs or those with young children in pushchairs. Motor traffic is confined to a short section between Swainsley and Redhurst, about half a mile below Wettonmill. Both the Tissington Trail and the High Peak Trail are also useful in this respect but the surface of the paths are not surfaced like the Manifold track.

For a 9 mile circular walk in the upper regions of both the Dove and Manifold Valleys, park in Longnor and take the path from Folds End Farm down through river meadows past Lower Boothlow Farm and on to Brund and then take the old packhorse route eastwards up the fields to Sheen. Cross the Sheen road by Lower House Farm and climb uphill to the ridge above Hartington where the path drops to a footbridge over the Dove before reaching Hartington by the side of the Stilton Cheese Factory. From the village take the gated road to Pilsbury and then the path past Pilsbury Castle and through river meadows to Crowdecote, which leaves a short stiff climb back to Longnor.

There are numerous old packhorse routes in the upper reaches of both the Dove and Manifold. These are now preserved as footpaths and are all marked on the White Peak OS map. If you have both the time and inclination they offer a wonderful opportunity to explore this little known area.

Additional Information

Craft Centres

Butterton
Manifold Arts & Crafts Centre
The Ford
Mellor Hall Old School
☎ (0588) 304320

Hartington
Rookes Pottery
Mill Lane
☎ Hartington (0298) 84650
Open: weekdays 9am-5pm,
Saturday 10am-5pm, Sunday
11am-5pm. Closed weekends in
January and February.
Terracotta garden pottery made on
the premises. Visitors may look
round the workshop and see pots
in production.

Longnor
Longnor Craft Centre
The Market Hall
Market Square
☎ Buxton (0298) 83587

Open: March-December daily
10am-5pm; January & February
Saturday & Sunday only.
Exhibits and sale of work by local
craftspeople and artists, including
traditional furniture.

Tourist Information Centres

Ashbourne
13 Market Place.
☎ Ashbourne (0335) 343666

Hartington
Hartington Railway Station
    (National Park)
No telephone.
Open: Easter-September. Saturday,
Sunday and Bank Holiday
Monday.

Ilam
Ilam Hall (National Trust)
nr Ashbourne.
☎ Thorpe Cloud (033 529) 245

3

THE SOUTHERN
LIMESTONE PLATEAU

M uch of the limestone district of the Peak lies south of Buxton, bounded to the west by the Dove and Manifold Valleys and to the east by the River Derwent. East of Buxton, the River Wye dissects the limestone as it flows to join the Derwent. The district bounded by these valleys is a flattish plateau with interlocking stone walls forming a grey patchwork on a green quilt, and dissected by a number of picturesque dales. Occasionally, the relief is augmented by clumps of trees or sometimes long lines of trees growing along the old lead mine veins and providing shelter from the wind, which cuts almost through you in winter. Dotted over the landscape are countless farms, some in small clusters and less frequently, grouped together in villages. It is almost a pattern for the district to see the ribbon development of the last two and a half centuries now welded into neat little villages. A good example of the linear pattern can be seen at Youlgreave and is met again in Sheldon, Chelmorton, Taddington, Elton, Bonsall, Winster and Wensley among others.

This is an area which the motorist seems intent on passing through as he rushes between the tourist centres that surround it. It is however, worthwhile seeking out its treasures, whether it be the dales of the Lathkill and Bradford, buildings such as Youlgreave Church and Winster Market Hall or the archaeological remains such as Arbor Low stone circle and the smaller circles on Stanton Moor.

The underlying feature of most of the district is the limestone, although east of Youlgreave, both Harthill and Stanton Moors consist of gritstone. Old quarries and lead mines abound and although the villages originally depended on a local well or spring for water, many of these have since dried up. Alteration in the water table from lead mining activities is often quoted as the cause, indeed, even some

ARCHAEOLOGY IN THE PEAK DISTRICT

As much of the land in the Peak District has never been ploughed, covered by forestry or urban development, it is an area rich in archaeological remains. Buxton Museum has particularly interesting dioramic displays of the area's prehistory. Many finds from the caves of the Manifold Valley are kept here. The Roystone Grange Trail, Britain's first archaeological trail, is a recommended pleasant walk, especially in summer, with remains from the Bronze Age to medieval times.

Among the oldest sites worth visiting is the Neolithic stone circle at Arbor Low, southwest of Monyash. Two others exist near Birchover — Nine Ladies Circle and Nine Stones Circle — where the stones are still upright.

Although there are no open chambered barrows or tumuli which can be examined — at least none on a public right-of-way — the Iron Age forts at Mam Tor and Carl Wark may be visited. Roman remains may be seen at Glossop and at Roystone Grange. Just north of the Snake Pass a Roman road survives, and this is also worth examining.

The Norman castle at Castleton is well worth the steep climb to reach it, and a fine Norman arch survives in Bakewell church, along with many other Anglo-Saxon and medieval stones. There are a number of other fine Anglo-Saxon crosses in the area. The best motte-and-bailey castle in the Peak is at Pilsbury, just north of Hartington, where an interpretation board shows how it may have looked.

Many of the tumuli in the Peak were excavated by Thomas Bateman, a Victorian 'barrow-digger', whose tomb — with a carved cinerary urn on the top — may be seen in Middleton-by-Youlgreave, situated in the corner of a field. Many of Bateman's finds, along with the more recent Heathcote finds from Stanton Moor are now housed in the Weston Park Museum, Sheffield. These include the Benty Grange helmet — a very important helmet from a christian Saxon warrior.

village ponds have suffered the same fate. In 1976, the River Bradford disappeared for several months, causing fears that the crystal clear waters had gone for good. Today, old lead mine drainage levels, or soughs (pronounced 'suffs') take a considerable amount of the surface water.

Despite the presence of limestone, the number of caves is surprisingly small, Lathkill Head Cave being the only one of any size. Early man made use therefore, of the surface of the area for burial purposes and numerous tumuli can be found marked on the OS map. It is little wonder that Thomas Bateman, the nineteenth-century barrow-digger, lived in this district, at Middleton-by-Youlgreave, and there are few of these 'lows' as they are called which escaped his attention. The most fascinating, and of national importance, is Arbor Low, situated south of Monyash, and just off the Youlgreave to Parsley Hay road. This huge stone circle, now in the care of English Heritage, consists of a ring of stones surrounded by a bank and ditch, the external diameter being nearly 300ft. It is now considered that the stones originally stood upright, although all but one have fallen, and that there were originally thirty-nine of them. Arbor Low has an evocative atmosphere. Adjacent to it is Gib Hill with an earlier henge. A Roman road runs just to the west of Gib Hill and an old trackway can be traced between the two. It would seem that the Roman surveyor made use of an already existing prehistoric trackway.

Stanton Moor, to the east, has an impressive collection of five stone circles and over seventy tumuli. The most celebrated circle is the one known as the Nine Ladies, which is not really a stone circle but the remains of a large barrow with the earth removed. The nine stones still stand, and with a further stone, the King Stone, situated some 130ft away. Many of these burial mounds and circles have been excavated and an impressive collection of artifacts has been created by the late J. P. Heathcote and his father, which may be seen at Sheffield Museum.

To the west, on Harthill Moor, lies another circle — Nine Stones, although only four stones now survive, together with the remains of an Iron Age fort, by Harthill Moor Farm. Nearby, a curious outcrop of rock is known as Robin Hood's Stride and the rocks nearby contain a small cave, used as a shelter by a hermit in medieval times. Between the rocks and the cave, is an ancient road known as the Portway. This was known to be an old trackway even in Saxon times and from the nearby fort it descended to Alport where it can easily be followed over Haddon Fields as it makes for Ashford.

A remarkable Anglo-Saxons artifact was found in the Benty Grange tumulus, just north-west of Arbor Low. Here, Thomas Bateman uncovered the burial of a warrior and his helmet consisting of iron straps with a silver cross affixed to the nose-guard and surmounted by a bronze boar. A further remarkable find came from a barrow at Winster which yielded a cross of pure gold surmounted by

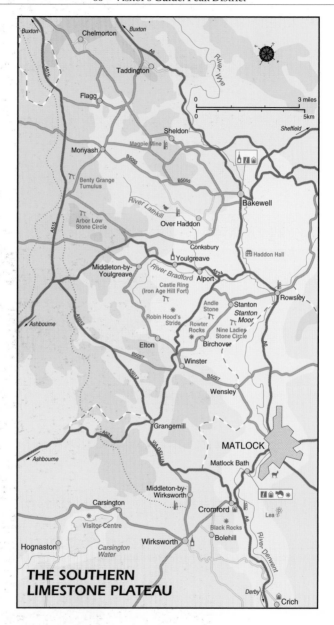

THE SOUTHERN
LIMESTONE PLATEAU

Lathkill Dale

*Walking in
Bradford Dale*

a cut stone of garnet. It is richly carved and denotes the Christian influence which was beginning to penetrate the area. This and numerous other artifacts can be seen in Weston Park Museum at Sheffield, which is well worth a trip on a wet day, particularly if you can combine it with a visit to Abbeydale Industrial Hamlet on the A621 (just before its junction with the B6375). Many of the tumuli, including Benty Grange, were excavated by Thomas Bateman who lived at Lomberdale Hall near to Middleton-by-Youlgreave. It is still a private house and is not open to the public. Nearby in the village of Middleton is the Congregational Chapel which he had built and at the rear (also on private land but visible from the road) is his grave. Surrounded by iron railings, the grave is covered by a stone tomb, surmounted by a carved stone cinerary urn similar to those he unearthed. It is a pity that his final resting place is largely unknown and forgotten.

DALES AND VILLAGES

The area covered by this chapter includes two of the most picturesque dales imaginable — Lathkill Dale and Bradford Dale. The clear waters in themselves are a striking attraction particularly when one has the time to watch the trout as they dart about. **Lathkill Dale** starts in an unpromising sort of way, half a mile to the east of Monyash. A footpath leaves the B5055 at the bottom of Bagshaw Dale and heads south-east towards Lathkill Dale. It is a convenient place to park the car. Soon, small outcrops of limestone give way to a narrow, deep and steep sided valley, devoid of water and with a rocky floor. After about a mile, the river can usually be seen flowing from the mouth of a large cave on the right, known as Lathkill Head Cave. Despite its promising proportions it is in fact a very low cave inside for a considerable distance before solution cavities lead down to other levels. It is also dangerous in showery weather with only a limited period to get out if prolonged rain suddenly sets in. Further downstream at the foot of the dry valley leading up to Haddon Grove, lie the remains of Carter's Mill. This small cornmill was intact during World War II but now only the foundations survive. Here, the valley becomes wooded and the path follows the river amid leafy glades and old lead mining ruins. In summer, with the sun dancing on the pure water of the river, it is a delightful spot.

Soon after entering the wood a weir dams the river creating a small pool with the occasional duck swimming about. This pool provided a head of water for two waterwheels lower downstream and the water course or leat can be seen running horizontally down the

WALKS IN LATHKILL DALE & BRADFORD DALE

This area contains some of the most attractive scenery in the Peak District and therefore the chance to spend a few memorable hours out walking should not be missed. A marvellous 6½ mile circular walk can be made involving both Lathkill Dale and its tributary the River Bradford. Park your car at the picnic area on Long Rake due west of Youlgreave (SK194645). Take the road towards Conksbury and upon reaching the third field on the left take the path to Meadow Place Grange. Proceed through the farmyard and cross the field to reach Meadow Place Wood where a track leads down to Lathkill Lodge and the River Lathkill. Take the path downstream to Conksbury Bridge and ensure that you look back at least once or twice, to catch the memorable sight of the water flowing over the many weirs a quarter of a mile above the bridge. Cross the bridge and almost opposite Conksbury Farm take the path which leads past Raper Lodge to Alport. Cross over the road to Youlgreave and take the path up the River Bradford. Below Youlgreave the first of six delightful pools of crystal clear water is reached. After passing the sixth climb out of the valley to Middleton and then take the path at the side of the road to Lomberdale Hall. At SK641199 take the path which crosses the road to Friden and climb up through the fields back to the picnic site.

The rest of Lathkill Dale should not be missed and for another walk (9½ miles) the path should be taken upstream from Lathkill Lodge towards Monyash. The first half of the valley is wooded and by and large this is also the most interesting part of the valley. The source of the River Lathkill is passed at Lathkill Head Cave before reaching Monyash. Return via the path from Manor House Farm which crosses Ferndale before reaching One Ash Grange Farm. From here proceed to the picnic area on Long Rake via Callinglow Farm and then return to Lathkill Lodge via Meadow Place Grange as described above. It should be noted that cars should be parked at the car park in Over Haddon and not at Lathkill Lodge.

valley on the far side of the river. Further downstream there are several collapsed shafts of the Lathkill Dale lead mine. The site of the 52ft diameter waterwheel — one of England's largest — can still be seen. Lower downstream, the leat crossed over the valley on an

FLORA OF THE PEAK DISTRICT

In the Peak District a large variety of flora can be found over relatively small distances. There are even areas of limestone heathland with soils sufficiently acidic to permit the growth of heather and bilberry. For example in the cutting where the High Peak Trail runs under the Ashbourne-Buxton road there are banks of purple flowering heather.

One of the most important sites in the Peak District is Lathkill Dale, where a variety of very different habitats may be found. However this is a very sensitive area and it is important to keep to the footpath. At the head of the dale, close to Monyash, where there is easy access to the valley sides, the land has been improved with lime. The pasture is lush and there is little floral diversity. After a couple of fields the valley sides become steeper, the slopes less amenable to improvement and the flora more diverse. Further into the dale the habitats north of the river differ from those to the south. The former catch more sun and there is more evaporation from the

The rare Jacob's Ladder growing in Lathkill Dale

aqueduct with limestone piers which have been preserved in various stages of completeness. This brought the leat to the northern side of the river where it ran to Mandale lead mine. Part of the engine house remains here, together with its associated pumping shaft, which also had a waterwheel for pumping purposes. The expensive-to-run Cornish-type beam engine would only be used when water power

soil. This draws up more lime, suiting calciole plants, with as many as fifty species per square metre in some locations. These warmer slopes attract sheep and the grass is shorter, encouraging rosette-forming species, which sheep find difficult to nibble. Ungrazed areas provide cover and food for invertebrates and small mammals. Among the screes the herb robert, shining cranesbill and false oat are more common.

To the south of the river the shadier soils receive less warmth and are moister and more acidic. Here the plants are lusher, taller, and there is more cover for mammals, reptiles and invertebrates. Even the woods downstream differ on each side of the river, more by hand of man than through natural causes. The valley is a fascinating example of several different complex habitats in close proximity to each other.

Of equal importance are the relict woodlands, survivors of the natural tree cover that existed before the land was cleared. Dovedale's ashwood is perhaps the best known of these. With the ash being the most common tree in the limestone dales the Peak does lack the rich show of Autumn colour seen elsewhere. Other examples of relict woods are the sesile oaks at Padley Wood near Hathersage and some areas of woodland around the northern moors (eg Jaggers Clough east of Edale). More unusual are the holly woods in the Hamps Valley south of Beeston Tor.

Additionally some plants have adapted to thrive in the special habitats around old lead mines, on the peat moors and the wetlands around the reservoirs, rivers and old canals.

Visitor pressure and the insiduous effects of acid rain take an increasing toll throughout the whole region. The National Park Authority, the National Trust and the county wildlife trusts all have interests in environmental conservation and tourist management in and around the Peak District. All welcome volunteers with time, expertise or finance to help preserve our natural heritage.

was insufficient. Much of the valley is part of the Derbyshire Dales National Nature Reserve. It is a sensitive area and visitors should not stray from the footpath. Leaflets about the reserve are available near Lathkill Lodge.

A few minute's walk from here is Lathkill Lodge with a mill pond and a former cornmill. From here one may climb out of the valley to

Over Haddon, where there is a craft centre, or southwards up the track and across the fields to Meadow Place Grange and Youlgreave. Unfortunately, the river bed is sometimes dry to this point which spoils the beauty of the spot. Downstream, a succession of eleven weirs creates a marvellous sight but one needs to walk upriver to sustain the benefit of the view. At **Conksbury**, the old packhorse bridge carrying the Bakewell to Youlgreave road is crossed before continuing down the opposite bank towards Raper Lodge. Surprisingly unmentioned by Pevsner, this handsome house looks down on the river and another old packhorse bridge. Raper Lodge was featured in the film *The Virgin and the Gypsy* starring Franco Nero. Also featured was much of Youlgreave which is referred to as Congreave in the story, written by D. H. Lawrence. Lawrence was no stranger to the area, for he lived for a while at Mountain Cottage, New Road, Middleton-by-Wirksworth.

The river meadows soon lead to **Alport** with its seventeenth- and eighteenth-century cottages, ancient bridge, and another mill and mill pool in an idyllic setting. Nearby the Lathkill meets the Bradford and closely hugs the road before meeting the River Wye at Picory Corner.

The River Bradford commences south of **Middleton-by-Youlgreave**, but the dale only becomes of consequence at Middleton where a track leads down to the dale. The track is a little rough underfoot and the bare limestone outcrops and overhanging trees give nothing away of the beauty of the dale beyond, as it brings one down to an old pumping station. The beauty of **Bradford Dale** lies in the six pools of crystal-clear water reflecting the mature trees, which line the sides of this steep sided dale at its upper end, downstream of the old pumping station. The track between Middleton and the river is a mass of yellow celandines in spring.

Youlgreave spills down into the dale, but the intrusion is a sympathetic one on the whole. A clapper bridge enables one to cross the river and either proceed downstream or walk up to the village. Beyond the bridge, the path hugs the river until a road crosses the valley, which by now is getting much more shallow and open. Just beyond the road a bridge crosses the river yet again and a path follows the river down to Alport.

A further valley worth having a look at is the **Via Gellia**. Unfortunately it now has the A5012 running down it, and is much frequented by heavy lorries. It is named after the Gell family who owned much land around here and lived at Hopton Hall. They planted the trees in the dale, for which it is well known.

This part of the Peak now has two long distance paths which run along former railway lines; the Tissington Trail (formerly the Ashbourne-Buxton railway line) and the High Peak Trail which follows the old track bed of the Cromford and High Peak Railway (C & HPR). The former railway was started in 1880 and closed partly in 1963, with the Hartington-Parsley Hay section closing in 1967. The 17 mile trail runs from Ashbourne (just north of the tunnel) and skirts the villages of Thorpe, Tissington, Alsop-en-le-Dale and Hartington before terminating just south of Dowlow Quarry near to Buxton. The old stations are now car parks and picnic areas, with an information centre in the former Hartington station signal box which is open to visitors during the summer weekends. In addition to the old stations near to these villages there are also car parks and picnic areas at Parsley Hay Wharf (where the Tissington Trail merges with the High Peak Trail) and at Hurdlow Wharf, on the Monyash to Longnor road.

The C & HPR was built to connect the Cromford Canal with the Peak Forest Canal and was built almost like a canal by a canal engineer. It was the only railway so built and it is not surprising to find long level sections interspersed with steep inclines (in lieu of locks) and stations known as wharfs. Apart from Middleton Top engine house, the signal box at Hartington, cuttings, embankments and inclines, there are few traces of these former railways other than the lines themselves, but the trails give easy access to a wide area of limestone countryside. The National Park hires out cycles at Ashbourne and Parsley Hay and perhaps this is an ideal way of getting about. Certainly enough people use the scheme and venture away from the nearby villages, perhaps to do a circular route. The level nature of the trails, while ideal for cycles, can become less than exciting for the rambler, although the High Peak Trail does offer more of interest, while sections of both are suitable for the disabled. If you have not ridden a bike for a while, you will find the High Peak Trail easier. It is flatter and surfaced with clinker rather than limestone. You will find it much easier to cycle north towards Parsley Hay on the Tissington Trail. If you are hiring your bike and making a circular trip, bear this in mind.

The first section of the 33-mile long C & HPR (from Cromford to Whaley Bridge) was opened as early as 1830, and was one of the earliest lines in the country. Today the 18 mile High Peak Trail stretches from High Peak Wharf on the Cromford Canal to just beyond Hurdlow Wharf. Access can be made to it at many places but perhaps the best are the old stations (or wharfs) at Hurdlow, Parsley Hay, Friden, Minninglow, Middleton Top engine house, Black Rocks

STONE WALLS

The Peak is characterised by thousands of miles of stone walls, which were mainly built at the time of the enclosures in the eighteenth and nineteenth centuries. Some are much older and a system of Roman walls as been discovered at Roystone Grange near Parwich. Quite often the walls preserve centuries-old farming patterns. Around Hartington the walls are known to follow the lines of the old strip-fields in considerable detail, preserving the field system as marked on a map of 1614.

The walls are dry, ie built without mortar. They are, in effect, two walls the middle being filled with small stones, but with plenty of large stones, or throughs, to bind the whole together. They are topped by large stones called 'copers'.

A good stonewaller never puts a stone down once he has picked it up. Competitions are held annually, but it is not a spectator sport!

Limestone walls are a distinctive feature of the White Peak

and High Peak Junction on the Cromford Canal. All of these places have a picnic area in addition to parking facilities.

An archaeological trail, starting at the Minninglow carpark (by the old railway bridge over the Parwich-Pikehall road), gives a fascinat-

Cycling on the High Peak Trail near Arbor Low

ing insight into the area's history. The Roystone Grange trail incorporates the old railway, a nineteenth-century brick kiln, the medieval Roystone Grange and an adjacent Roman farmhouse and field system. An inexpensive leaflet on the trail is available from the National Park office at Bakewell.

If you park at Minninglow (SK194582) cross the road and walk 1½ miles through a plantation towards Friden, where the old railway has a bend in the line near a farm. This is the Gotham Curve, in its day the tightest curve on British Railways, which turned the line through 80 degrees! Further to the east at Hopton is one of the old inclines, originally worked by a stationary engine which hauled up the locomotives on a cable. This gradient was easier to tackle than the others on the line and the more modern and powerful locomotives could get up it unassisted. It was the steepest gradient worked on British Railways without assistance. It can easily be reached by taking the Wirksworth road from Brassington or alternatively the road to Hopton from the Via Gellia valley. Middleton Top Engine, situated high above Middleton-by-Wirksworth village, still retains the beam engine that hauled the locos and wagons up the Middleton incline. It is usually open on Sundays and is in motion on the first Saturday in the month. It is a unique survivor of the very early railway era. It is easy to find because of its tall chimney.

If a walk along the plateau stretch of the line is thought to be lacking in interest, then try the 1¾ mile section from Black Rocks on the Cromford to Wirksworth road down to the Cromford Canal. Either arrange for someone to take a car around to the bottom, as there is a considerable drop in altitude, or walk a circular route to return to the car. A suggested 7 mile route is to follow the canal to Whatstandwell. On the way you pass the beam engine which pumped river water up into the canal. At Whatstandwell cross the river and take the path that runs westwards from a little north of Hankin Farm until the road is reached on Wirksworth Moor. This should be followed northwards to Bolehill and Black Rocks. This route gives one an opportunity of examining the buildings which survive at the High Peak Junction, together with the catchpit near the bottom of Sheep Pasture Incline — complete with a railway wagon which ran away and was 'caught' in this safety device.

In addition to the dales there are, of course, the many villages which are scattered thoughout the area, chiefly in a linear pattern on the limestone plateau. They all have their own characteristics and space only permits a mention of some of them. In the north, **Chelmorton** lies besides a large hill, presumably on the site of a spring; it is an interesting place to examine. The oldest part of the village was obviously near to the hill and spring, which is why the church and pub now appear to be at the end of a cul-de-sac. With the coming of the first enclosure, land appears to have been allotted so that each cottage had a few strips behind it and this order has been preserved, so that even today there are many narrow fields stretching away; later enclosures resorted to a more regular pattern.

To the south-west lies **Monyash**. It was once an important centre of the lead mining industry, with a weekly market. Its old market cross still stands on the green, its base supposedly made from the old village stocks. The lead mining area of Derbyshire still has its own Barmoot Court — the oldest industrial court in the country, possibly a thousand years old. There were several courts, which are now all held together at Wirksworth, but formerly Monyash and Winster had their own. The dependence of the area on agriculture is also expressed in the large village pond or mere. There were formerly four in the village but only one, Fere Mere, remains. The pub is very popular with walkers and tourists, particularly in the summer as one can sit outside facing the village green.

Youlgreave is typical of the Peak District linear villages, with its sturdy church, displaying architecture spanning 800 years, standing in a dominating position at the end of the main street. It is an ideal spot from which to explore the Lathkill and Bradford Dales. It too was an important lead mining village and its many houses are old workers' cottages. Youlgreave Hall, standing close to the road, reminds one of Hartington Hall but lacks the grandeur of the latter's setting, although they are comparable in age. The village is fortunate to have several shops, although the old Co-op is now a youth hostel. Look for the old circular stone water tank, or conduit head of 1849, built to provide a head of water when a public supply was first brought to the village. It is opposite the youth hostel.

To the south lies **Winster**, with a similar history of dependence on lead mining, demonstrated by the discovery of a water pressure engine in a nearby mine, now re-erected in the Peak District Mining Museum in Matlock Bath. It had originally been built at Coalbrookdale in 1819 for the Alport mines, near to Youlgreave, before being moved to Winster nearly 30 years later. Look for the Market Hall in the centre of the village, which was the first property acquired by the National Trust in Derbyshire. Pevsner describes it as being of the fifteenth or sixteenth century, but its original open ground floor arches have been built in with brick to give it more stability. It is open to the public and the National Trust maintains a small display on the

MERES

The limestone plateau is an area mainly devoid of surface water. Rain water for animals and villagers was captured in clay-lined ponds known as meres. Most villages had one, usually fed by a spring or stream, and many exist in open fields. Each farmer would bring his animals to drink at a specific time in the day.

Monyash had four meres, some for animals and one for domestic use. The largest, Fere Mere, still survives. Some meres are very old, for example Heathcote mere, near Hartington, was in existence in 1482.

Fere Mere, Monyash

first floor. In the main street lies the early Georgian hall, now a hotel.

Robin Hood's Stride (or Mock Beggar's Hall) is a gritstone outcrop, most readily viewed from the A524 Winster to Alport road. Two 'chimneys' give the impression of a large building, especially at dusk. At the foot of the nearby Cratcliffe Tor is a medieval hermit's cave sheltered by an ancient yew tree. There is a crucifix carved on the wall and a niche for a lamp. The Portway, one of the Peak's oldest trackways, passes nearby. To the north is Nine Stones Circle, with the tallest standing stones in the region, although only four survive. The nearby Castle Ring is a large Iron Age hillfort, but it is difficult to

Youlgreave Hall

The Earl Grey Tower on Stanton Moor

appreciate its size as the path runs below the ramparts.

To the north of Winster are the Rowter Rocks at Birchover, which were once thought to have Druidical connections, hence the name of the nearby Druid Inn. Caves, rooms, steps, alcoves, armchairs, etc, were carved from the rocks to form a retreat for the local vicar, the Rev Thomas Eyre who died in 1717. However the huge rocking stone no longer rocks.

Depending on time a drive around some of Winster's neighbouring villages should not be overlooked. There are some delightful corners to be seen in **Stanton-in-the-Peak** and **Birchover**, just to the north. The stone circles and Bronze Age tumuli on Stanton Moor have already been mentioned, but look out for the Cork Stone, Cat Stone and Andle Stone — huge natural blocks of gritstone, the latter having footholes and iron handles for climbing to the top. The sharp-eyed visitor might find the rocks with dates and initials that were carved in the early nineteenth century by the Thornhill family of Stanton Hall. More obvious is the Earl Grey Tower, built in 1832 to celebrate the passing of the Reform Bill.

To the east on the minor road from Wensley to Matlock via Oaker Hill, lies the tiny village of **Snitterton** with its lovely hall. There are many places of interest like these if one is prepared to go and seek out the backwaters.

Reference has already been made to the former lead mining activities. Old shafts abound in the area; indeed a current estimate is that as many as 100,000 shafts are scattered throughout the Peak. Many are, of course, shallow and blocked at the surface; others are deep; many are dangerous but only if not treated with due respect.

The region's lead mining museum is situated in Matlock Bath and the area now under discussion contains some of the deepest and richest mines in the Peak. The most notable remains are those of Magpie Mine near to **Sheldon**. They can be seen from the Monyash to Ashford-in-the-Water road and details of access can be obtained from the Peak District Mining Museum although a footpath crosses the site. The remains have been preserved, including the remains of a Cornish-type beam engine house, two chimneys, headgear, the winding drum of a steam whim and much else. A full description of the mine layout can also be bought from the museum. The remains of Mandale Mine in Lathkill Dale can also be visited.

Opencast mining for fluorspar occurs from time to time, often reworking the waste heaps thought worthless by the old lead miners, but as the sites are worked out the land is restored to agricultural use. Also worthy of mention is the limestone mine at Middleton-by-

Wirksworth, being worked for a pure type of limestone used in the refining of sugar.

Between Middleton-by-Wirksworth and Bolehill is the National Stone Centre. Situated on a 50 acre site, it explains the story of the use of stone from prehistoric times to the present.

Off the Cromford to Wirksworth road at Bolehill is the Black Rocks Trail. There are three woodland trails around the **Black Rocks** outcrop, a picnic area plus a walk on the High Peak Trail. The gritstone rocks here are popular with rock climbers.

Just north of **Middleton-by-Wirksworth**, on the A5012 Cromford-Newhaven road is Good Luck lead mine, which has been turned into a mine museum, and although it is still being explored and old passages dug out a lot of workings may be seen. It is open to the public but only if you are definitely prepared for it and are not claustrophobic. The passage is narrow in places, low in others, but gives a good impression of a typical lead mine of the area. Enquire at the Peak District Mining Museum in Matlock Bath for opening details (usually the first Sunday in the month).

To the south of the region lies **Wirksworth**. It would be easy to dismiss it as a drab town set amid the devastation of centuries of mining and quarrying but there has been much conservation work here recently and there are several interesting buildings which are worth seeking out. The church is hidden behind the shops and several narrow passages give access to it. Even the main gates to the church are hemmed in between shops. The church contains a richly carved stone coffin lid of about AD800, found under the floor in 1820. Even though incomplete it depicts forty figures and is regarded as one of the most interesting early Anglo-Saxon remains in Britain. The churchyard is circular in shape — an indication of a very early Christian settlement.

If time does not permit a visit to the church, a path circles the churchyard creating a backwater of peace and quiet. Walk around the north side of the church past the old Grammar School, founded in 1576 and rebuilt in 1828 in a neo-Gothic style. Its battlements and pinnacles create a pleasing elevation worth looking at; it is now used for furniture manufacture. Continue past the old almshouses and turn north with the latter and the Grammar School on your left, to emerge into Coldwell Street. On the right is the old manse, a three-storey Georgian building standing opposite the older, early seventeenth-century Manor House, hidden behind its hedge.

Near the top of Coldwell Street, towards the Market Place, a passage on the right of the United Reform Church leads into Chapel

The ruins of the Cornish engine house at the Magpie Lead Mine, Sheldon

Wirksworth church

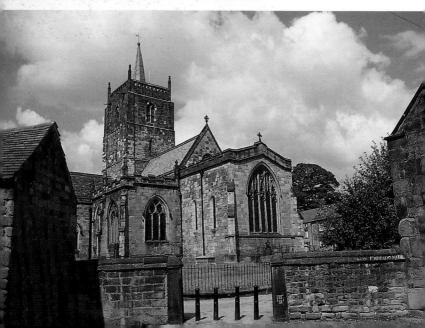

Lane. On the left, some 200yd or so up the lane stands the Moot Hall, which was rebuilt in 1814. It still houses the standard measure for lead ore — a bronze dish made in 1513. At each sitting of the Barmoot Court the jury receive tobacco to smoke after their meal. As the

Saxon carving of a lead miner in Wirksworth church

The new visitor centre at Carsington Reservoir

twentieth century draws to a close Britain's oldest industrial court still purchases clay pipes for its members to smoke their tobacco! Return to Coldwell Street past the imposing Red Lion pub and cross the main road. Have a look at Symonds House (Number 15) across the road from the Red Lion, together with the restored seventeenth-century former house behind it in Dale End. Climb up the lane to reach Babington House on the left. It is a stiff climb up Greenhill to it but the house is well worth seeing. Pevsner attributes it to the early seventeenth century, although on a modern porch is the date 1588. Near the town centre is a heritage centre where local customs and industries are explained, along with other aspects of the town.

To the west of Wirksworth is Carsington Reservoir, opened by HM the Queen in 1992. There is a visitor centre, a cycle hire centre, a watersports centre with hiring facilities and a footpath which can be used in conjunction with local roads to provide a circular walk of approximately 9 miles. The visitor centre is open every day, even at Christmas, and is a popular attraction in the area.

North of Wirksworth, and in the Derwent Valley lies **Cromford** which grew as a result of the prosperous mill of Sir Richard Arkwright. Arkwright built the Greyhound Inn together with houses for his workers and a school for their children. North Street, on the south side of the road to Wirksworth, was built by him and the school is situated at the end of the street. Behind the Wirksworth road and just to the east of North Street is the village lock up and the 'tail' or beginning of Cromford Sough. The water is piped across the A6 and was used to supply water to Arkwright's Mill, crossing Mill Lane by the mill on a cast iron aqueduct dated 1821, and to the Cromford Canal. The mill is being developed as a museum and there is a shop and café here.

It was at Cromford that Sir Richard Arkwright established the world's first water powered cotton mill in 1772, which survives in modified form on the Crich road at SK298569. Arkwright also built Masson Mill, situated alongside the A6 between Cromford and Matlock Bath, in 1783. It is still proudly displays the legend 'Sir Richard Arkwright & Co, Established 1769'. The old cornmill on the A5012 to Newhaven situated at the edge of Cromford village has also been preserved.

Down Mill Lane, the road to Crich, there are a number of features also of interest. After passing under the 1821 aqueduct and by the side of the canal basin it passes the church built by Arkwright. If you look back across the basin, you can see Rock House where he lived.

From the Cromford Canal basin there is a pleasant towpath which leads to High Peak Wharf with its buildings from the Cromford and High Peak Railway. Vehicle access can be made to a car park off the Cromford-Lea road, where the latter turns to the left away from the Derwent Valley. A path crosses the river and runs adjacent to a sewage works to reach the canal and wharf. In the buildings here can be seen a section of the world's oldest in-situ railway line. It dates from 1828 and carries the inscription 'C&HPR'.

Just down the canal from here is the Leawood Pumping Station, which used to pump water from the river to the Cromford Canal. It is now fully restored, including a 50in diameter cylinder Cornish-type beam engine and plunger pump which is steamed periodically. This huge engine, dating from 1858, is well worth a visit, and is a worthy monument to its builders and to the time and patience of its volunteer restoration team. Ask at local information offices for details of steaming days.

Cromford Bridge is fifteenth-century with rounded arches on one side and pointed arches on the other! At the Cromford end is an early eighteenth-century fishing temple, almost identical with Walton and Cotton's in Beresford Dale, and the ruins of a bridge chapel. On the parapet of the bridge a cryptic inscription records the successful leaping of the parapet by a horse and rider in 1697. Across the bridge is the entrance to Willersley Castle; now a Methodist guest house it was built by Arkwright but he died in 1792 prior to its completion. The road keeps close to the river before turning towards Lea Bridge and **Holloway**. The latter was the home of Florence Nightingale, who lived at Lea Hurst, now an old folks' home, but occasionally it may be visited on open days. A few years ago a firm of Bakewell solicitors opened a long forgotten box and were intrigued to find it contained some of her possessions. **Lea** was also the home of Alison Uttley who was born at Castle Top Farm. When the rhododendrons are in flower in May and June it is worth visiting Lea Gardens. An old quarry was planted with timber and rhododendrons over 50 years ago. Today the different species of rhododendrons are mature and a truly wonderful sight. The scent of the flowers pervades the whole wood and the colours of the flowers have an amazing variety and beauty.

The road up the hill at Holloway affords some good views over the Derwent Valley towards the white painted Alderwasley Hall. A diversion of a mile or so leads to the outskirts of **Crich** and the tramway museum with its national collection of trams. There are over forty vehicles including a handful from overseas. They vary from a horse-drawn Sheffield tram of 1874 to another Sheffield tram

INDUSTRIAL ARCHAEOLOGY

The most noticable industrial remains are the 100,000 or so lead mine shafts, which are to be found mainly along the worked out mineral veins. Derbyshire's lead mines were worked from Roman times, and in the seventeenth and eighteenth centuries large quantities of lead were used on the roofs of churches, country houses and other buildings. The mineral veins are often easy to identify as they often have a long belt of trees to act as a windbreak. The most complete mine complex is at Magpie Mine northeast of Monyash, while another ruined enginehouse is at Mandale Mine, in Lathkill Dale. The Peak District Mining Museum at Matlock Bath displays many artifacts and a huge pumping engine, powered by water pressure, recovered from deep underground near Winster. Lead mine shafts are dangerous and one should satisfy one's curiosity about them from a safe distance.

The huge steam engine at the Leawood Pumphouse on the Cromford Canal

There is plenty to interest railway enthusiasts. The world's oldest *in situ* piece of rail can be seen at High Peak Wharf near Cromford, together with other buildings and incline-hauling equipment. Buildings remain at the Hulme End terminus of the Leek and Manifold Valley Light Railway. The Froghall incline, abandoned in 1920, was the second oldest line in Britain and may still be followed in places. Various other lines have been converted into trails. Railway centres exist around the peak at Cheddleton, Foxfield, Glossop and Butterley. The National Tramway Museum at Crich houses over forty restored trams which now operate on a mile-long track.

Canals surround the Peak and survive to this day, although the Cromford Canal has been abandonded following a tunnel collapse. Canal wharfs remain at Buxworth, Whaley Bridge, Marple, Cromford and Froghall.

Stationary steam engines were usually sold off, but the region is fortunate in having two preserved in situ, and both open to the public. Middleton Top winding engine hauled waggons up an incline on the Cromford and High Peak Railway, while a Cornish-type beam engine worked a huge plunger pump at Leawood on the Cromford Canal.

The Peak has few water mills, although the Brindley Corn Mill at Leek, and Cheddleton Flint Mill are both open to the public. Caudwell's Mill at Rowsley is a preserved roller-driven corn grinding mill which now has a craft centre and a small tea room. The large complex of mill buildings comprising Arkwright's mill at Cromford is also now preserved. Unfortunately it still lacks a good interpretative feature on cotton spinning and is devoid of machinery, unlike the Paradise Silk Mill at Macclesfield (where demonstrations take place on the original weaving machines). Cromford village has much else of interest, including early examples of houses built by Arkwright for his workers, and a trail leaflet is available.

Scattered along the gritstone edges above the Derwent Valley are many abandoned millstones and grindstones. Below Surprise View near Longshaw are hundreds of them, many still stacked ready for removal along an old tramway line. On the limestone area are some very good examples of old limekilns, ranging from quite small examples built just to satisfy local needs, to large batteries of kilns, the largest being at Froghall Wharf.

of 1950, which was the last one in the city when the service finished in 1960. The car park ticket entitles you to ride on one of the selection of trams which are operated on the mile or so of track down the edge of a quarry and beneath Crich Stand, a monument to the Sherwood Foresters who fell in the two World Wars.

A trip to Crich can usefully be left for a rainy day for there is much to see and much can be done even when it rains. The tram sheds can be visited as well as a museum which is housed behind the façade of the old Derby Assembly Rooms. With much Victoriana preserved in a street scene, you can lose yourself in a past age and wonder how long it must be before there is a tramway revival.

When you take your tramride, look out for the lead mining display erected by the Peak District Mines Historical Society. You can get off to look at this and get another tram back. Lead ore was smelted in the area of course, initially in bole hearths which required wind for draught and later in cupolas which were an early reverberatory furnace. One such cupola existed at Stone Edge about 9 miles due north of Crich at SK334669. The chimney still stands and it is the oldest free-standing industrial chimney in Britain, dating from about 1770.

Upriver from Cromford is **Matlock Bath**, a mecca for many visitors to this area. It is a place full of hustle and bustle, crowds and souvenir shops, but not for those who come to the Peak District for the beauty and peace of its hills and dales. The A6 becomes choked with cars on sunny Bank Holidays. Not surprisingly, there is much to see, so allow plenty of time and a full wallet. One of the more recent additions is the Mining Museum, run by the Peak District Mines Historical Society. The centre piece of its exhibits is a huge water-pressure engine found in a mine at Winster. This is an interesting, not a stuffy museum, and while you interest yourself in the exhibits, children can explore simulated passages and shafts.

A dramatic addition to the attractions at Matlock Bath opened at Easter 1984. Now visitors can take a cable car ride up to the Heights of Abraham. This gives a spectacular and unique view of the Derwent Valley. The cable car station is a little upstream of Matlock Bath Railway Station. It is easy to locate by looking for the cables slung over the A6 and the River Derwent. Elsewhere in the town there is Gulliver's Kingdom, for young children, and there are several show caves and mines. The Rutland Cavern at the Heights of Abraham (actually an old mine not a cave) has a very good display involving a model of an old miner who explains working conditions in his mine and the Peak District Mining Museum has opened the old

Temple Mine for visitors too. There is a good range of shops, a promenade above the river and a railway station. Each year, Matlock Bath has its illuminations with illuminated floats on the river and a firework display. More details on dates can be obtained from the information office next to the Mining Museum.

A further new addition to the attractions here is the Whistlestop Visitor Centre, in some of the old railway buildings adjacent to the station. Here the Derbyshire Wildlife Trust has established a nature centre which is well worth a visit. On a similar theme is the Riber Castle Wildlife Park, established in the grounds of the mock castle which dominates the skyline south of Matlock. It is now a fauna of British and European animals and birds.

Upstream from Matlock Bath railway station are the High Tor Grounds — 60 acres in extent with walks and views down into the Derwent Valley, with the river nearly 400ft below. Access is from Dale Road or Church Street, Matlock or just upriver from Matlock Bath railway station.

Just south of Matlock Bath is the New Bath Hotel. Most people tend to regard it as being purely residential, but it is not. When you begin to flag a little from 'doing the rounds' in Matlock Bath, it is an excellent choice for coffee and biscuits. **Matlock** itself is a good shopping centre, but it lacks the architectural appeal of Buxton, Bakewell or Ashbourne, for example. Fortunately its shops are on the flat, for much of the town itself overlooks the river.

Matlock developed as a spa town and many hydros, or more correctly hydropathic establishments, were built in the mid-nineteenth century. The last major hydro to survive was Smedleys, which finally closed its doors in 1955. It is a massive structure and is worth having a look at. It is now the County Council Offices and was built by John Smedley, who also built Riber Castle which dominates the skyline to the south of the town. The castle's huge structure cost him £60,000.

In addition to the canal, there was also a railway up the valley as far as Rowsley, where it headed up the Wye at the Duke of Devonshire's insistence that Chatsworth had to be spared the intrusion of a railway. The railway exists only as far as Matlock now, although planning permission has been granted to the Peak Rail Society to relay the track and run trains to Darley Dale. Matlock formerly had a tramway and a couple of trams used to run up and down the steep hill (Bank Road) between the Crown Square roundabout and Smedley's Hydro, now the County Council Offices. The tramway was closed down in 1927 and the tram shelter which stood on the site

Rhododendrons at Lea Gardens

Boarding a restored tram at the National Tramway Museum, Crich

High Tor at Matlock Bath

The Victoria Tower and the start of the cable car ride across the Derwent valley, at Heights of Abraham, Matlock Bath

of the roundabout was moved to the adjacent gardens where it can still be seen.

There is not a great deal to detain the tourist upriver of Matlock before Rowsley, apart from a possible diversion to the left at Darley Dale to visit the Red House Stables Carriage Museum.

Additional Information

Places to Visit

Crich
The National Tramway Museum
nr Matlock
☎ Ambergate (0773) 852565
Open: April-September daily, except some out of season Fridays. Collection of about fifty trams from home and overseas. Unlimited rides on 1½ miles of tram tracks.

Cromford
Arkwright's Cromford Mill
Mill Lane
On minor road leading to Lea and Holloway, 200yd east of Cromford crossroads on A6.
☎ Wirksworth (0629) 824297
Open: daily 9.30am-5pm, closed 25 December.
The world's first successful water-powered cotton spinning mill, now owned by the Arkwright Society undergoing complete restoration. Exhibitions, audio-visual display and guided tours available.

Good Luck Mine
Via Gellia, SK270565
Opened: first Sunday in every month. Details from Peak District Mining Museum, Matlock Bath.
☎ Matlock (0629) 583834
A typical small lead mine.

High Peak Junction Workshops
High Peak Junction, nr Cromford
Signposted off A6 in Cromford.
☎ (0629) 823204
Open: Easter to October, weekends, Bank Holidays; June, July to mid-September, daily 10.30am-5pm. Restored railway workshops of Cromford and High Peak railway. Displays, video, model working forge, shop.

Leawood Pumping Station
☎ Wirksworth (0629) 823727
1849 beam engine, fully restored and steamed periodically. Enquiries to Leawood Pumphouse c/o Middleton Top Visitor Centre Wirksworth, Matlock, DE4 4LS
☎ 0629 823204

Lea
Lea Gardens
☎ Dethick (0629 534) 380
Open: mid-March-end July, daily 10am-7pm.
A rare collection of rhododendrons, azaleas, alpines and conifers in a lovely woodland setting.

Matlock
High Tor
Access from near Matlock Bath station, Church Street or Dale Road, Matlock or from Starkholmes.

Open: daily, 10am-dusk.
60 acres of grounds, walks and extensive views.

Riber Castle Wildlife Park
Situated off A615 at Tansley, via Alders Lane for 1 mile to Riber.
☎ Matlock (0629) 582073
Open: daily from 10am (closed Christmas Day)
World famous Lynx collection; home of rare breeds and endangered species. Cafeteria, picnic areas, gift shop. Magnificent views over Derwent Valley. Licensed bar.

Red House Stables Carriage Museum
Darley Dale
☎ (0629) 733583
Open: daily from 10am.
Over forty horse-drawn vehicles, equipment and harness rooms.

Matlock Bath
Gulliver's Kingdom
Temple Walk
☎ Matlock (0629) 580540
Open: Easter-October, 10.30am-5.30pm daily.
Turn up the hill to the south of and opposite the Pavilion.
Party rates available. Staff help available for wheelchairs on the slopes.

Model Village and Children's Fantasy Land.
Heights of Abraham
Adjacent to Matlock Bath railway station
☎ Matlock (0629) 582365
Open: Easter-end October, daily, 10am-6pm (later in high season).
Cablecar; Great Masson Cavern and Pavilion; Visitors' Centre; Victoria Prospect Tower; Great Rutland Cavern and Nestus Mine; Alpine Centre.

Matlock Bath Aquarium
North Parade
☎ Matlock (0629) 583624
Open: daily in summer and weekends in winter, 10am-5.30pm.

Peak District Mining Museum
The Pavilion
☎ Matlock (0629) 583834
Open: daily except Christmas Day 11am-4pm (later closing summer).
Trevithick's giant water pressure engine. Climbing shafts and tunnels. Displays of geology, minerals and mining in the Peak District since Roman times. Shop selling souvenirs, specialist mining books and local interest books.

Royal Cave
☎ Matlock (0629) 580540
Adjacent to Gulliver's Kingdom and only accessible on an inclusive ticket from there.
Open: Easter-end September, 10am-5.30pm. Party rates available.

Temple Mine
Details of visits may be obtained from the Peak District Mining Museum at Matlock Bath.
☎ Matlock (0629) 3834

Whistlestop Countryside Centre
Old Railway Station
☎ (0629) 580958
Open: April-October daily 10am-5pm. Winter Saturday & Sunday 12noon-4pm.

Winster
Market House
Open: April-September 10am-4pm.

Wirksworth
Middleton Top Engine House
Middleton Top, Wirksworth
Signposted off the B5036 Cromford to Wirksworth road.

☎ Wirksworth (0629) 823204
Open: Easter to October, 10.30am-5pm, Sundays (engine static); first Saturday in month and Bank Holidays (engine operating). Restored beam engines built in 1829 to haul waggons up a $1:8\frac{3}{4}$ incline on the Cromford and High Peak railway.

National Stone Centre
Porter Lane
☎ (0629) 824833
50 acre site telling the story of stone from prehistoric times to present. Open: all year.

Wirksworth Heritage Centre
☎ Wirksworth (0629) 825225
Open: April-July Tuesday-Saturday 10.30am-4.30pm, Sunday 12.30-4pm; August to mid-September 10am-5pm. Reduced opening in February, March mid-September-December.
Situated in the an silk and velvet mill. Local customs and industries explained, with recreation of the life of a quarryman in the early 1900s. Computer game and Dream Cave for children. Restaurant and craft workshops.

Craft Centres

Grangemill
Nigel Griffiths
Old Cheese Factory, in Via Gellia on road to Winster
☎ Winster (0629) 650720
Open: Monday-Saturday, 9am-5pm. Hand-made oak furniture.

Kirk Ireton
Peter and Kate Spencer
The Riddings Farm
Overlooking Carsington Reservoir
☎ Ashbourne (0335) 370331

Open: workshop all year; nursery October-October daily 10.30am-7pm or dusk if earlier.
Furniture restoration, cabinet making, upholstery and wood-working courses. Small nursery specialising in herbs, alpines and unusual plants.

Lea
The Coach House
☎ (0629) 534346
Open: all year 10.30am-6.30pm and 7-11pm.
Craft shop, farm shop with home-made paté, cheese, yoghurt etc; famous home-made Jersey ice cream, tea rooms, restaurant and accommodation (B & B and self-catering).

Over Haddon
Lathkill Dale Craft Centre
Manor Farm
☎ (0629) 812390
Open: daily 10am-5pm.
Ceramics, furniture, clocks, stained glass, art, bookbinding. Tea room.

Wirksworth
T. C. Jones (T/A Frank Pratt)
Church Walk, Wirksworth
☎ Wirksworth (062 982) 2828
Open: Monday-Friday, 9am-5pm, Saturday, 9am-12.30pm. Saturday pm and Sunday by prior arrangement.
Hand-made, hand-carved furniture can be viewed being made.

Tourist Information Office

Matlock Bath
The Pavilion.
☎ Matlock (0629) 55082

4

THE NORTHERN LIMESTONE PLATEAU

The River Wye rises on Axe Edge and flows down to Buxton before turning eastwards to divide the limestone region into two. Its deeply cut valley does this quite effectively and today much of its course north of Rowsley is followed by the A6 trunk road. The valley has two quite distinct features. North-west of Bakewell it is narrow and deeply incised with sheer limestone bluffs which even overhang the river in places. It is joined by many tributary valleys, mostly quite deep but chiefly devoid of water: Great Rocks Dale, the two Deep Dales, Monks Dale, Tideswell Dale, Cressbrook Dale and Taddington Dale being the largest. Southeast of Bakewell, the river flows across softer, later rocks which have eroded more easily creating a wider valley.

Fortunately, the A6 road took advantage of Taddington Dale and so spared perhaps the most beautiful part of the Wye, between Topley Pike and the bottom of Monsal Dale. Part of this can be viewed from the car, but much is preserved for the rambler, including the most interesting parts of Chee Dale, Water-cum-Jolly Dale and parts of Monsal Dale.

North of the Wye, the limestone plateau is dissected by some of the tributary valleys mentioned above. The limestone upland stretches as far north as Castleton and Eyam (which are included in Chapter 5) and includes some minor hills such as Longstone Edge, Bradwell Moor and Eldon Hill. It is an area of dry-stone walls and dry valleys with dairy and sheep farms. It has been an important area for quarrying and lead mining too.

The area was also of importance to man in early times. When the Romans arrived they found a small, but presumably effective, system of Iron Age forts and routes connecting them. The ancient

Portway which came north from Derby crossed through the area. From Wirksworth, the road headed via Grangemill for Castle Ring, an Iron Age fort northwest of Winster above Robin Hood's Stride. From there, it made for Alport and crossed the high ground west of Bakewell before descending to the village of Ashford-in-the-Water where it forded the Wye. It is easy to see the Portway at Ashford descending down to the river opposite Ashford Hall. Ashford was an important crossing place of the River Wye and the ancient Portway was used for centuries as a major highway. Indeed, north of the village, it is now tarmac-covered and is still in use as part of the road to Wardlow and Foolow.

The importance of Ashford is reflected in the establishment of a castle north of the church although nothing now remains except for a few place names, including Castlegate, the current name for the Portway north of the village. From Ashford, the Portway proceeded to Monsal Head along the existing roadway and then on to Wardlow Mires where it probably branched, heading through the fields to an Iron Age camp at Burr Tor, close to the gliding club, and then on to Bradwell via Robin Hood's Seat. The alternative route from Wardlow Mires took a more direct route to Bradwell via Windmill. Somewhere along the road between Ashford and Monsal Head, a track would have branched off to the west to the Iron Age fort at the top of the promontory known as Fin Cop. There is no public right of way to the fort but the site can be best appreciated from the west of the River Wye. Fin Cop is visible for a considerable distance and with its two very steep sides at almost right angles to each other it would have presented a visually impressive and physically important defensive position. It is perhaps best photographed from the west, a good vantage point being from Taddington village.

Of great antiquity even in Iron Age times were the tumuli and stone circles. Just to the north of Tideswell is Tideslow, the largest tumulus in the Peak District. Perhaps of more interest is Five Wells, unfortunately off the right-of-way, just north of the farm of that name situated on the path between Chelmorton and Taddington, as it crosses Sough Top. The tumulus can also be seen from the A6 near the Waterloo public house, standing out on the skyline. Five Wells is a chambered burial tomb, from the Bronze Age, which was uncovered during excavation. It is apparently the highest cairn in the country at 1,400ft, and relics from here and other prehistoric sites can be seen in Buxton Museum.

Buxton, Bakewell and the Wye Valley

Buxton itself has an ancient history. It attracted the Romans because of its warm mineral water which bubbles up to the surface. They built a bath here and called their settlement *Aquae Arnemetiae*. To the bath came Roman roads from Derby, Leek, Brough (*Navio*) east of Castleton, and south from near Glossop from a fort probably called *Ardotalia* but more popularly known by the fictitious *Melandra*. Other roads came from the west and the north-west. A Roman milestone found in 1856 is now preserved in the museum.

After the Romans left, the spring was not entirely forgotten and by Tudor times it had a reputation for curing invalids. Mary, Queen of Scots, while a prisoner in the custody of William, Earl of Shrewsbury, came here to seek relief from rheumatism. The Crescent, built adjacent to the spring, was designed by John Carr of York for the fifth Duke of Devonshire. It was built between 1780 and 1790 and was the first important imitation of the Royal Crescent at Bath, as part of a deliberate plan by the Duke to build Buxton into a spa town to rival Bath. Its cost, according to Pevsner, was £38,000 which means it could have been financed out of a single year's profit from the Ecton Mine in the Manifold Valley, as is traditionally believed. It was built primarily as a hotel and shopping complex and was partly occupied from 1786. At the north end was the Great Hotel, until recently the public library. The library was worth a visit, particularly to the Assembly Room upstairs to view its restored and decorated ceiling, but its future is, at present, uncertain.

Patronage by the Devonshire family continued with the building of the stables to the rear of The Crescent during 1785-90. This was converted to the Devonshire Royal Hospital in 1859, and the central courtyard for exercising the horses was covered with a dome in 1881-2. At the time, it was the largest dome in the world, being 156ft in diameter and weighing 560 tons!

Adjoining the Crescent were the thermal and natural baths; the latter at the south end and the former at the northern end. The thermal baths have been converted into a shopping complex, retaining some features of the old baths. Behind the Crescent are the Pavilion, Opera House and Pavilion Gardens. The gardens and conservatory are worth a visit, as is also the restored Opera House, which has a high reputation for the quality of its performances. The Buxton Festival is held annually during July.

Opposite the Crescent the former Pump Room is now the Buxton Micrarium. This is the world's first 'planetarium of the microscope',

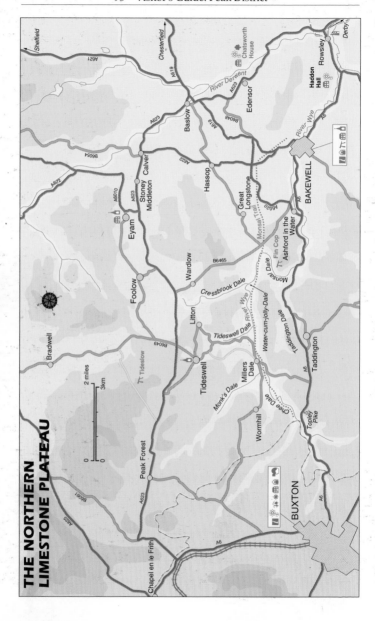

THE NORTHERN
LIMESTONE PLATEAU

The Pavilion Gardens, Buxton

allowing visitors to explore for themselves this fascinating world. The Buxton Museum and Art Gallery in Terrace Road includes archaeological remains found locally, fine examples of objects made of Blue John stone from Castleton and Black Marble from Ashford-in-the Water. Of special note are the excellent dioramas showing life in prehistoric times — complete with sound effects. There is much else to see in Buxton. A walk down Spring Gardens, the main shopping street, is recommended. The town, one of the highest in England, has a railway station, good bus services and municipal conveniences such as the Pavilion Gardens, bowling greens and two golf clubs. It also has a youth hostel at Sherbrook Lodge, set amid the trees opposite the hospital.

South of the hostel and the town, on Grin Low, is Solomon's Temple. This folly was built to provide labour for out-of-work men. It is worth visiting if only for the panoramic view over Buxton. Northwards lies the high moorland of Combs Moss and Shining Tor; to the south-west is Axe Edge, and south-eastwards can be seen Sough Top and the green fields and grey walls of the White Peak. The neat fields and clumps of trees of the limestone area contrasts vividly with the rugged treeless moors of the western edge of the Peak.

Northwest of Buxton, at Whaley Bridge, is the basin of the Peak Forest Canal, where an old warehouse, limekilns, etc remain. Canal enthusiasts should visit the imposing staircase locks at Marple Bridge, where there are more warehouses, while at the bottom of the locks is a large aqueduct some 80ft high over the River Goyt.

The northern portion of the limestone region has many similarities to the area south of the Wye Valley. A rolling landscape of green fields with an intricate system of dry-stone walls is synonymous with the Peak District limestone region as a whole. Other than the River Wye itself however, the area is devoid of any river system. It is, of course, bounded in the east by the River Derwent, but this flows through the gritstones of the eastern edge.

There are no counterparts for the river systems of the Dove, Manifold, Lathkill and its smaller tributary, the Bradford. The presence of several dry valleys has already been indicated and while pleasant enough, they lack the attractions that flowing water can create. The most interesting dale therefore is that of the Wye. It is crossed by a road at Miller's Dale, there is a minor road to Litton, and a road to Cressbrook and Wardlow Mires drops into the dale at Monsal Head. A little further south, the A6 runs up the valley to the bottom of Taddington Dale and returns to it for the section between Topley Pike and Buxton. There is much to see on foot and fortunately the linear pattern of the valley can be overcome by catching a bus back to one's starting point if the need arises. Buses run between Buxton and both Tideswell (for Sheffield) and Bakewell (for Derby and Chesterfield).

Topley Pike (SK103725) offers a good place to start. One can park opposite Tarmac's quarry at this point, where a minor road turns down to the river. It is marked on the OS White Peak map. This track follows the river down to the bottom of Great Rocks Dale, where ICI's quarry has the longest working face in Europe. The track passes through well wooded surroundings, sharing the narrow valley with the railway which crosses three times overhead. Upon reaching the footbridge and the row of cottages — presumably built for workers of the disused quarry behind — one also leaves Wye Dale for **Chee Dale**. Below here, the dale becomes much more interesting and in wet weather, even adventuresome!

For most of the way, the path hugs the river, but in places it becomes precipitous particularly where it runs on the south side of the river near to the railway arch, and also just upstream from the tributary Flag Dale. The valley is characterised in places by sheer limestone bluffs, several of which overhang the valley bottom. In two places, this forces the path into the river and onto stepping stones. If the river is in flood, the dale can be quite impassable. The outcrop of limestone, some with sheer waterworn slabs and over-hangs, offer considerable sport to climbers. The valley is well wooded in places which offers some variety of scenery. It would be easy to overstate the scenery of the dale, but if you sometimes get bored with the near-regularity of the beauty and riverside paths in some of the other dales, remember Chee Dale.

A little beyond Flag Dale, the valley opens out a little as one approaches the footbridge carrying the path from Wormhill to Blackwell over the river. Beyond here it is just a short walk into **Miller's Dale**. In former days Miller's Dale was an important place locally. It not only served as a railway station for many surrounding villages, including Tideswell, but Manchester to Derby through trains stopped here to pick up passengers from Buxton. The passenger traffic, together with the limestone traffic, made Miller's Dale a big station for its location. The Tideswell-Taddington road crosses the valley here too and river, road and railway are neighbours yet again. There are in fact, two quite impressive railway bridges situated side by side, the initial bridge being augmented in 1903 by the second one, 40 years after the line opened. Commerce also dictated a road down the dale at this point to serve Litton Mill. Originally it

The limestone uplands at Chelmorton

The church at Millers Dale

The tranquil River Wye at Water-cum-Jolly Dale

Monsal Dale Viaduct

was a waterwheel driven cotton mill, and textile manufacturing has only recently ceased. The mill earned a reputation for the unfortunate excesses of child labour in the early nineteenth century, epitomised in Walter Unsworth's novel *The Devil's Mill*. The path down the dale proceeds through the millyard, where the road ends.

Beyond here lies **Water-cum-Jolly Dale**. One wonders whether the impounded water, backing up from Cressbrook Mill, inspired the name or whether it dates from a time prior to this. On a summer's day the broad expanse of water with the waterworn limestone bluff behind reflecting in the millpool and the occasional duck or moorhen on the surface adds to the tranquillity of the dale.

Cressbrook Mill no longer operates. The main four-storey structure which dates from 1815 replaced an earlier mill built by Arkwright in 1779. Of interest is his apprentice house by the mill race, looking like a Gothic castle, with narrow lancet windows and turrets. Today this elegant mill crowned by a cupola looks forlorn, but it is slowly being restored. On the south side of the mill, more recent additions add little of aesthetic value. Downstream from the mill the path follows the lane to Monsal Head. Do not take the first bridge across the river, but the second, situated where the road begins to rise towards Monsal Head. The path goes through the arches which carried the railway line to Buxton from Bakewell. Ruskin strongly objected to the intrusion of the railway, but the line has mellowed into the landscape and the viewpoint from Monsal Head is now, ironically, well known and popular with photographers. Just downstream from the railway arches the River Wye tumbles over a weir which many people must recognise from the numerous postcards and calendars in which it features. From here the path cuts through the meadows at the bottom of the wood to meet the A6 at the foot of **Taddington Dale** where there is a picnic site, car park and toilets.

Below Taddington Dale, the river meanders slowly to Ashford-in-the-Water and Bakewell. A footpath follows much of the route, passing through Great Shacklow Wood, emerging by the river close to where the water flowing down Magpie Sough reaches the Wye. The sough (pronounced 'suff') drains Magpie Mine, situated over a mile away south of Sheldon village. The entrance or sough-tail is new and gated, the old entrance having been re-opened after being in a collapsed state for several years. The path is an easy walk amid a leafy glade, reaching the fields by an old watermill. There are three waterwheels here; two are attached to the mill buildings and there is a third and much smaller one which was used to pump water up to

Sheldon village before mains water was laid.

After a short walk through the fields the path reaches Kirkdale and the road to Sheldon. The works depot at Kirkdale used to be a marble mill and many of the black marble slabs visible in Derbyshire churches were cut and polished here. The stone, which is really a dark limestone which takes a high polish and looks like marble, was mined from two localities nearby. Not far away was found a rare red-coloured deposit of limestone and occasionally examples can be found in local churches. The marble works lost some of its buildings when the Ashford bypass was built, which spared the village much heavy traffic. **Ashford-in-the-Water** is worth a look around, particularly to view the old packhorse bridge — Sheepwash Bridge — and its neighbouring pump shelter, although the village pump has now gone. The village was once of at least equal importance to Bakewell, but that has all changed now. As early as the seventeenth century, 300 packhorses, laden with malt, passed northwards through the village each week.

Bakewell is the central town of the Peak and attracts many thousands of visitors. It has interesting groups of buildings and a good selection of shops, both for provisions and souvenirs. Its bookshop carries a wide range of books and papers on the Peak District. Several shops offer Bakewell puddings, preserving the memory of the culinary accident that produced the new dish. The disaster apparently occurred at the Rutland Arms when the cook put the jam at the bottom of the dish instead of on top of the pastry as is usual.

Although much of Bakewell is comparatively recent, as much building took place from late Victorian times onwards, the town centre does have some fine buildings which are worth looking at and some are quite old. The National Park Information Office is situated in the former Market Hall which dates from the early seventeenth century. Rutland Square — where the roundabout now is — was set out in 1804 when the Rutland Arms was built. This is a fine coaching inn and its stable still remains across the road, the buildings being built around two courtyards, one behind the other.

The Bath Gardens adjacent to the Rutland Hotel stables used to be the gardens to Bath House built by the Duke of Rutland in 1697 over a natural spring. Bath House is the last building on the left at the Bath Street end of the gardens and is now occupied by the British Legion. The duke's bath still survives in the cellar and is 33ft by 16ft in extent! Bakewell failed, however, to develop as a spa town like Buxton and Matlock.

THE MONSAL TRAIL

Parts of the former railway between Buxton and Rowsley have been developed into the Monsal Trail. The 9 mile trail commences in the north at Blackwell Mill Cottages at the top of Chee Dale and in the south, at Coombs Road Viaduct south of Bakewell. At Blackwell Mill Cottages, instead of crossing the river, a footpath leads uphill to the old railway. Follow the track and after about one mile, a tunnel is reached which is unsafe and a descent must be made to the river. At the time of writing it is probably best to regain the trail at Miller's Dale station. A further two tunnels below Litton Mill must also be bypassed by crossing the river over the footbridge near the mill, and following the river down to Upperdale. Here a road crosses the river and the railway may be rejoined near Putwell Mine, identifiable by its small chimney.

After crossing the famous railway viaduct over the River Wye, it is necessary to leave the line due to another tunnel. Climb out of the valley up the steps to Monsal Head. From here, take the road to Little Longstone, and a path back to Ashford to the rejoin line. There are no further difficulties to Bakewell. This is a useful trail despite the the tunnels and it enables one or two circular routes to be planned which were not possible before. Currently, the track is still surfaced with railway ballast. Although the other trails in the Peak may be used by the disabled, cyclists or horses, this trail is not recommended at the present time for these.

Sheepwash Bridge, Ashford-in-the Water

Bakewell has many interesting old buildings

Behind the hotel is a small area of old houses which reward investigation. Just up the road to Monyash is the old town hall on the right, one of the most interesting buildings in the town. Behind is the church, situated on an elevated site with its steeple dominating the skyline. There are two ancient crosses in the churchyard, of the ninth and eleventh centuries. The one beneath the eastern end of the church was found in Two Dales, north of Matlock.

The church itself dates from Norman, possibly Saxon, times. Much of the structure had been built by the end of the fourteenth century and Pevsner regards the accumulated headstones and coffin slabs, housed in the south porch, as the largest and most varied group of medieval monuments housed in the United Kingdom. They were found during restoration work in 1841-2. Some of the stones date from the Anglo-Saxon period and these presumably include the scroll work in pieces to the right as one goes through the porch. More of these carved stones can be seen on the west wall of the nave. Bakewell church is well worth a look around.

To the west of the church is the Old House Museum. It was built in 1543 and has been restored by the Bakewell Historical Society. Just to the north of the church is Bagshaw Hill, and halfway down is Bagshaw Hall, built in 1684. To the rear is Bakewell Youth Hostel, built in the hall's former kitchen garden. To complete a circular tour of the town centre, cross the A6 at the bottom of Bagshaw Hill and walk past the Millford Hotel to the mill leat of Victoria Corn Mill (which still has its iron waterwheel in the millyard, having been lifted out of the wheelpit for restoration but now sadly decaying). Turn downstream and follow the leat to Castle Street which brings you out by the bridge over the River Wye which was built in 1300. Just a little upstream is Holme Bridge, a packhorse bridge built in 1694 and now a footbridge. There is a sheepwash and interpretation board at the A6-road end of the bridge.

Perhaps the main point of interest of Bakewell is that it acts as a centre for visiting different parts of the Peak and of course the two major houses of the area — Chatsworth and Haddon Hall. The latter lies just down the river from the town and is a must for any visitor. It is very much older than Chatsworth, and is claimed by many to be Britain's most complete non-fortified medieval house.

Haddon Hall stands adjacent to the A6, hidden by trees and a beech hedge. The car park is across the road, so that one approaches the gatehouse on foot. The entrance is impressive with two lines of mature beech hedges converging at an old packhorse bridge over the wide but shallow waters of the River Wye. The house itself stands on

COUNTRY HOUSES

The Peak District was never rich enough to support many large country houses and they are comparatively few in number. The richer agricultural land around the Peak supported more large houses, but a number in the southwest have been demolished. These include Beresford Hall near Hartington, as well as Ilam Hall and Throwley Hall, both in the Manifold valley. Beyond the park boundary, we no longer have Ashbourne Hall (except for a fragment, as at Ilam), Osmaston Manor, Calwich Abbey, Wootton Hall and Snelson Hall, all near Ashbourne, as well as Highfield and Ashenhurst near Leek.

Despite this loss the area has four houses of national importance, and all open to the public. Chatsworth House, one of Britain's most visited stately homes, is renowned for the quality of its interior and collections as for its Palladian west front. There is much to see here and a full day is not really long enough.

Close to Chatsworth is Haddon Hall, perhaps the most complete medieval non-fortified house in England and a home of the Duke of Rutland. To the east of the national park is the Elizabethan Hardwick Hall, overlooking the M1 motorway and now owned by the National Trust. The house was built by Bess of Hardwick, the founder of the Cavendish dynasty, headed by the Dukes of Devonshire. From a more recent era is the work of Robert Adam at Kedleston Hall (also owned by the National Trust), northwest of Derby, with some of Adam's finest interiors.

On a smaller scale is Eyam Hall, which first opened its doors to visitors in 1992. It is the only village manor house open to the public within the national park. The early nineteenth-century Hassop Hall is now an upmarket hotel and its restaurant is recommended. Callow Hall, near Ashbourne, is smaller and is also now a good hotel and restaurant.

Other houses worth visiting are those on the western side of the Peak: Lyme Hall near Disley with its Palladian south front and older north front. Near Macclesfield are Adlington Hall which is similar, although the north wing is fifteenth century, Capesthorne Hall, a huge pile rebuilt by Salvin after a fire, and the smaller Gawsworth Hall, a delightful black and white timbered house with parts dating from 1480.

Near to Hardwick Hall are Bolsover Castle and Sutton Scarsdale, both owned by English Heritage. The latter is completely roofless and the former partly so.

Haddon Hall

a bluff overlooking the river and the bridge, although somewhat masked by the trees, and the entrance is at the foot of the north-west tower with a very low doorway.

The battlemented buildings are set around two courtyards paved with flagstones. In the south-west corner of the hall and lower courtyard is situated the chapel. This is probably the oldest part of the hall for parts of the chapel were built by William Peveril around 1080-90. The altar slab in the south aisle of the chapel is of Norman origin as are the two fonts in other parts of the chapel. It has a three decker pulpit and various pews built by Sir George Manners in 1624. The chapel is very well lit by natural means and remarkably well preserved. It contrasts greatly with the chapel of Chatsworth which is resplendent in all its richness.

The old kitchens are on the left of the entrance to the banqueting hall and still retain such items as bowls carved into the wooden bench tops. Beyond the kitchen is the bakehouse and butcher's shop which provided essential food for the house. The entrance hall opens into the banqueting hall which was built around 1350 by Sir Richard Vernon, and this is essentially as he built it with oak panelling and a large open fireplace. The minstrel's gallery was added later, however. The long table in the hall is 400 years old and contrasts with the roof above it, which had to be replaced in 1924. Even so the new roof is a genuine attempt to recreate the style of the old. Off the banqueting hall is the dining room which dates from 1500 and was

The lower courtyard, Haddon Hall

added by Sir Henry Vernon. This is a delightful room with much carved panelling showing the coat-of-arms of the Talbot family and Edward VI when Prince of Wales.

Above the dining room on the first floor is the great chamber with a remarkable number of tapestries plus moulded plaster work. In a succession of rooms the visitor's notes advise of architectural details dating parts of the building to around 1500 or even earlier. Haddon Hall is an amazing survival, in a very good state of repair, of this period of English architecture. The long gallery with its heraldic glass window dated 1589, beautifully carved stone mullions, and panelled walls carved as long ago as the middle of the sixteenth century make this one of the most beautiful rooms in the house. The room also has a delightful painting by Rex Whistler, painted before his famous mural at Plas Newydd on Anglesey. It shows the house, the Duke of Rutland (who restored the house) and his son — now the current duke.

Haddon Hall is, of course, famous for the love story concerning Dorothy Vernon. Her elopement in 1563 with John Manners was immortalised by Sir Walter Scott, and just off the long gallery one can still see the steps down which she is supposed to have fled, meeting her lover at the little packhorse bridge below the gardens. Unfortunately, the story is as ficticious as it is romantic, as the long gallery and adjacent garden were built by John and Dorothy 26 years after their marriage. Unless of course, it was from a previous building on the site. We shall never know, but at least it keeps the story alive! In the latter half of the seventeenth century the Duke of Rutland moved his family seat to Belvoir Castle in Leicestershire, so that for well over 200 years the hall became more or less empty and unused, although still maintained. This is the reason why the hall was never 'restored' or rebuilt. Today it represents a microcosm of life in a country house over four hundred years ago.

Just below Haddon lies **Rowsley**. Here, the Lathkill joins the Wye at Picory Corner and the combined waters flow towards the Derwent. Rowsley is a small village: the surprising thing about the place is that it is not much larger. It used to boast a substantial railway marshalling yard — a relic of the days when Rowsley was the rail head of the Midland Railway's line from Derby and prior to the building of the connection with Buxton which began in 1860. It boasts a very fine hotel, the Peacock, originally built in 1652 and which later became a dower house of Haddon Hall. Of particular interest to residents and visitors alike is a ceramic peacock just inside the entrance. It is one of five made by Minton of Stoke-on-Trent in

1850-1, and this one went down with the ship *Loch Ard* in 1878, 14 miles off Moonlight Heads, Victoria, Australia. It was brought up during salvage operations, and eventually came back to England. Minton have apparently traced four of their peacocks and a visitor from Australia told the hotel that she had number five, also brought up from the hapless *Loch Ard*. At Rowsley the River Wye joins the Derwent, flowing south from the northern gritstone moors past Calver and Chatsworth. Rowsley also has a working museum at Cauldwell's Mill. This roller driven corn mill was rescued by a group of friends who maintain it. Visitors are welcome and there is a tea room and craft centre.

At Rowsley the River Derwent can be followed upstream to Chatsworth Park where there is a convenient free car park at Calton Lees, which can be used to visit the Chatsworth Garden Centre, or to walk to Chatsworth through the park and alongside the river. Alternatively there is a car park at the house itself. (Chatsworth is described in Chapter 6.)

North of the Wye

The limestone region north of the River Wye is an interesting one. It is a patchwork of small villages and undulating farmland cut by deep valleys, such as Cressbrook Dale, Coombs Dale and Middleton Dale. To the east it is overlooked by Longstone Edge, with the scar of High Rake Mine. The latter was once the scene of the worst financial lead mining venture in the whole of the Peak and is now an opencast site, worked more recently for fluorspar rather than lead ore.

Apart from Eyam, which is situated on the edge of the gritstone and is reserved for a later chapter, the largest village is **Tideswell**. There must be many visitors to the Peak who miss — or drive straight through — Tideswell. With its multitude of shops — including a Co-op, a chemist, two restaurants, banks and filling station — it can offer most things a visitor needs. It is a medley of small buildings in rows and little nooks. It even has a gas supply, to the envy of many other Peakland villages.

The area around the church is a pure gem, even though at first glance it does not give the impression of being anything special. Park near the church and have a look at the George Hotel, a fine coaching inn with Venetian windows and dating from 1730. To the rear of the church is the vicarage and at its side, the library, a superb example of vernacular architecture, combining cut blocks of limestone with gritstone quoins and mullions.

The George Inn and church, Tideswell

The village stocks at Wormhill

The fifteenth-century cross at Wheston, west of Tideswell, was (like Foolow cross, below) probably a boundary marker of the former Royal Forest of the High Peak

Foolow village and its medieval cross in a mantle of snow

WALKS IN THE AREA

There is a 6 mile walk with plenty of interest north of Bakewell. Park near Holme Bridge at SK215690 and take the path to the rear of Lumford Cottages. It climbs up through a small plantation adjacent to Holme Bank Chert Mine before cutting across the fields in the direction of Great Longstone. Just north of the little cottage known as Cracknowle House, the path leaves the fields and descends through Cracknowle Wood to Rowdale House and the A6020 from Ashford-in-the-Water to Hassop Station. Turn left towards Ashford and walk along the road to the junction of the various roads adjacent to the old railway bridge. There is an access road from this junction to Churchdale Farm and on towards Churchdale Hall. The path skirts around the plateau and then drops down a hillside to rejoin the A6020. Walk down the footpath at the side of the road and turn left on the old and now disused section of the B6465. This has now been re-routed and crosses the River Wye over a new bridge. Upon reaching the A6 a path cuts across the fields on your left and to the north of the A6. There are views towards Ashford Hall and down onto Ashford lake which runs into the large mill pond of Lumford Mill. This has created quite an elongated and interesting sheet of water in the valley below the path. Eventually one walks towards a group of houses and the path cuts through the middle of the development to join the A6 once more close to Lumford Mill. There is a short walk down the path at the

Fortunately for visitors, a leaflet gives a concise history of the church for there is much to see. There is a wealth of different brasses, some very old, including one showing Bishop Pursglove of Hull who was a native of Tideswell, in full eucharistic vestments as worn before the Reformation. The original building was enlarged in the fourteenth century and is very impressive; it is certainly a must for the discerning visitor and fully lives up to its title of 'Cathedral of the Peak'.

Elsewhere, the villages follow the familiar pattern, either elongated or set around a village square. Most are very small but with little features here and there that make a visit worthwhile — the stocks in Litton; the fourteenth-century cross and adjacent village pond in Foolow; the memorial to James Brindley, the canal engineer, at Wormhill where he was born, all spring to mind. East of Litton, on

side of the A6 to Holme Bridge. Here the former sheep wash has been restored and there is an interpretation board which details changes made to the river over the centuries to provide water both for Lumford and Victoria Mills.

There is a 10 mile path which enables the walker to enjoy the variety offered in a somewhat dry, ie riverless, Derbyshire dale and also on the limestone plateau above it. Park at Peak Forest and take the path which leads towards Dam Dale Farm and into Dam Dale. The path continues on down a rather long valley which heads towards the River Wye at Miller's Dale. It has several names after leaving Dam Dale, the next is Hay Dale followed by Peter Dale and Monk's Dale. Parts of this valley system are now part of the Nature Conservancy Council's Derbyshire Dales National Nature Reserve. Consequently great care should be taken not to interfere with the wildlife or stray from the footpath. Upon reaching Miller's Dale, just beyond the church a track leads off uphill. It is marked unsuitable for motor vehicles. After climbing out of the valley and above Monk's Dale Farm it joins an old green lane which runs directly to Weston. Part of it has been tarmaced but the rest is comfortable walking. The road continues north-west of Weston in the direction of Peak Forest. At SK128778 a track leads off to the left. A footpath is soon reached which should be taken back into Dam Dale towards Dam Dale Farm and Peak Forest.

the road to Wardlow Mires is the top of **Cressbrook Dale**, its steep sided valley coming right up to the road. A pronounced feature of this end of the valley is Peter's Stone which is a detached block of limestone of significant size. It can be viewed from the A623 at Wardlow Mires, but the signposted footpath from there down the top of the dale enables you to get quite close. It is also the outcrop depicted with a wheatear on the front of the first edition of the White Peak OS Map.

Mention of the fourteenth-century cross in **Foolow** has been made above. It is worth more than a passing glance; indeed much can be missed by not stopping and having a look around. The cross was resited on the green in 1868 at the rear of a flat stone with an iron ring set in its top surface. The stone is a bullbaiting stone and must be very old, for bull baiting was made illegal in 1835. The cross stands by the old village mere, fed by a spring with a wall around it. Around this centre sit the village school, manor house, pub, and chapel and other old village buildings dating from the seventeenth and eighteenth centuries. Although Foolow looks a small village of little interest, this is not the case, as perhaps the above indicates. This is not confined to this one village for there is much to be found in most of the Peakland villages, if you care to seek it out.

A network of footpaths enables you to explore some of the area on foot. Tideswell is a good centre from which to start exploring. For instance, take the road towards Tunstead and after descending into the top of Monk's Dale, which is now a nature reserve, a path cuts up through the fields to Wormhill reaching the village by the church. At the southern end of the village, at SK124729, take the path which heads south and then south-eastwards descending into Chee Dale. Follow the path downstream to Miller's Dale and then take the riverside road to Litton Mill. Just before the mill, turn up Tideswell Dale, beneath the grounds of Ravenstor Youth Hostel. On reaching the B6049 walk the last mile or so up the road into Tideswell. Total distance about 7 miles.

Additional Information

Places to Visit

Bakewell

Haddon Hall
☎ (0629) 812855
Open: April-September daily except Mondays 11am-6pm (also closed Sunday in July and August). Totally unspoilt medieval and Tudor manor house with magnificent terraced rose garden, set in the beautiful valley of the River Wye.

Old House Museum
Cunningham Place,
off Church Lane
Open: Good Friday-end October daily, 2-5pm. Parties booked for morning or evening visits
☎ Bakewell (0629) 813647.
Folk Museum in historic early sixteenth-century house, once owned by Sir Richard Arkwright and partitioned to house some of his workpeople.

Buxton

Buxton Micrarium
The Crescent
☎ Buxton (0298) 78662
Open: late March-October, daily 10am-5pm. February & March Saturday & Sunday only 11am-4.30pm.
Exhibition of nature beneath the microscope. Forty-four remote controlled microscopes projecting onto TV-sized screens.

Buxton Museum and Art Gallery
Terrace Road
☎ Buxton (0298) 24658
Open: Tuesday-Friday 9.30am-5.30pm, Saturday 9.30am-5.30pm.

Extensive collections of geology, archaeology, prehistory and local history relating to the Peak District. Temporary monthly art exhibitions.

Peak Rail
Buxton Steam Centre
☎ Buxton (0298) 79898
Steam Centre open: all year except Christmas and New Year, 10am-5pm. Steam rides: Easter and May Bank Holidays; Sundays and some Saturdays in April, May and June; all Saturdays and Sundays in July and August plus August Bank Holiday; Sundays in September and October 1.30-5pm.
Many special events; also Peak Rail Rambler on the scenic route from Buxton to New Mills on summer Sundays and August Bank Holiday Monday.

Pooles Cavern & Buxton Country Park
Green Lane
☎ Buxton (0298) 26978
Open: Easter-end October, daily, closed Wednesday (except high season) 10am-5pm.
Beautiful natural show cave; 100 acres of woodland with nature trail, free car park, picnic area, toilets, shop.

Craft Centres

Bakewell
Cameron Pearson
Coulsden Cottage,
Bath Street

☎ Bakewell (0629) 813919
Open: weekdays (except Tuesday am) 9am-5pm, also Saturday am.
Founders of letters and signs in cast aluminium, brass and bronze.

Rowsley
Caudwell's Mill and Craft Centre
☎ (0629) 734374 (mill)
or 733185 (craft centre)
Open: March-October daily 10am-6pm, November-February Saturday & Sunday 10am-4.30pm.
Historic water-powered flour mill, café, gift and craft shop, working crafts including wood turner, glass blower, potter and clockmakers. Wholemeal flower always available.
Guided tours by arrangement (including evenings) in summer.

Tideswell
Chapel House Furniture
☎ Buxton (0298) 871096
Makers of English oak furniture and smaller items of domestic woodware.

Tourist Information Offices

Bakewell
Old Market Hall (National Park)
☎ Bakewell (0629) 813227
Open: daily except Thursday in winter.

Buxton
The Crescent
☎ Buxton (0298) 25106

5

THE DARK PEAK

North of the limestone region lies the Dark Peak. Strictly speak
ing it includes the area of the Upper Derwent Valley and the
moors east of there, but for convenience these have been included in
Chapter 6. It is really an unfortunate description, for it connotes a
forbidding area, and although there are areas of desolate moorland,
much of it is not. Indeed, the gritstone regions which surround the
limestone include some of the best scenery in the area, whether it be
around the upper Dane, the Churnet, Stanage or the northern area
under discussion here. In fact, many will incline to the view that the
Dark Peak is of more interest than the limestone district further
south. In addition to the great expanse of peat moors such as Kinder
Scout and Bleaklow, there are the less rigorous walking areas of the
Hope and Edale valleys separated by the ridge between Lose Hill
and Mam Tor, with the isolated Win Hill situated at the end of Hope
Valley and blocking the east-west trend of the Edale Valley. Here can
be seen some of the best countryside that the Peak has to offer.

To the south lies Bradwell at the neck of a valley between the
somewhat featureless Bradwell Moor and Bradwell Edge which
dominates the village. Beyond is Abney Moor and Eyam Edge where
the gritstones drop steeply to the limestones and the White Peak.

This is an area of significant historical interest. The Iron Age
hillfort on Mam Tor commands an impressive position and sits
astride a routeway possibly as old as the earliest colonisation of the
Peak. Later the Romans established a fort at *Navio*, near Brough,
north-west of Bradwell. Their roads stretched away to Buxton, along
Doctor's Gate to *Ardotalia* and eastwards towards Sheffield. Relics of
their occupation can be seen in Buxton Museum. Later, a Norman
castle was built nearby, giving its name to the settlement below it —

Castleton. The keep still survives, together with much of its perimeter wall. All around are the relics of the once important lead mining industry and hundreds of shafts pockmark the landscape. Beneath Mam Tor is the Odin Mine, traditionally said to have been worked by the Saxons. There is no evidence to prove this, but it all helps to create the impression of antiquity in the area.

On the moors, the early lines of communication have remained relatively intact, especially the possible Roman road known as Doctor's Gate. Whatever its age, this narrow track is an amazing relic and a watchful eye needs to be kept to ensure its preservation. The track is actually named after Dr John Talbot, an illegitimate son of the Earl of Shrewsbury who was the vicar of Glossop from 1494 until 1550. Presumably he would have used the road when travelling from his home to his father's castle at Sheffield. The track is 3 to 5ft wide and can be seen to advantage on Coldharbour Moor, where the original paving slabs and kerbstones are intact.

Further Roman roads can be traced in this area such as the road from *Aquae Arnemetiae* to *Ardotalia* (Buxton to Glossop) and a good account of them is given in *Peakland Roads and Trackways* by A. E. and E. M. Dodd. Of more recent origin are the numerous packhorse routes which cross the area, many making useful footpaths such as the Edale to Castleton path via Hollins Cross which can be traced on the OS map in its entirety. Alternatively, north-west of Hope Cross, the Roman road which is now a bridle path crosses Blackley Clough where other hollow ways can be seen, now completely disused, but worn down over centuries of use. The legacy of these old roadways is an important network of paths which enable us to explore the area thoroughly.

Of equal interest are the remains of early settlements. There is little to see at the Roman forts of *Navio* at Brough and *Ardotalia* at Glossop (erroneously referred to by the fictitious name of *Melandra*). However, it is possible to walk around the site of the latter. It is a rectangular site and the stone foundations have been excavated. Looking around it is clear just how commanding a position the site occupied. Mam Tor's Iron Age fort, apparently built around the fifth century BC, is more interesting. Its dominating position above the impregnable south-facing cliff of Mam Tor is impressive in itself, with magnificent views down the valleys. For the curious, however, the ramparts remain except where the vertical cliff facing Castleton has eaten into the hillside. You can park close to the fort at the car park on the Edale-Castleton road at Rushup Edge (SK124833). Mam Tor and the Winnats form part of the National Trust's 30,000 acre

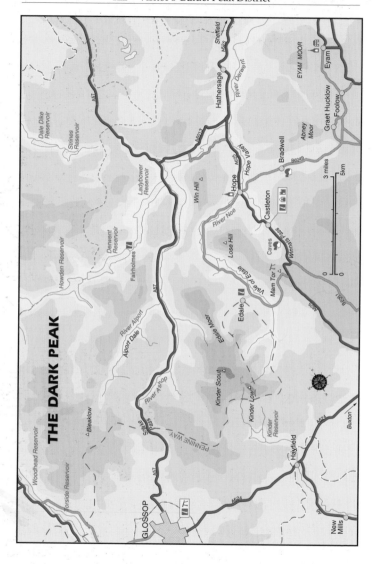

The Plague Cottages, Eyam

Eyam Hall

High Peak Estate, which also includes much of the 'Dark Peak'.

Below Mam Tor sits Castleton, on an outpost of limestone worked for centuries for lead and Blue John stone and now for cement. Above the village is its castle on a site reminiscent of Mam Tor with its sheer drop and protected flank. The sheer drop is to Cave Dale which perhaps gives the most impressive view of the castle keep, looking across the dry valley. The alternative view, of course, is from the village, but this lacks a degree of perspective, having to view it from below. The castle was built by William Peveril, the illegitimate son of William the Conqueror, in 1080, as a wooden stockade. This was later rebuilt in stone and the stone keep was added in 1175. The castle was only one of several in the Peak, others existing at Bakewell, Ashford-in-the-Water, Hathersage and Pilsbury, north of Hartington, but these were minor affairs and Peveril Castle was by far the most important. It seems to have been a hunting lodge of the Royal Forest of the High Peak and Henry II happened to be here when he received the submission of King Malcolm of Scotland in 1157.

The Plague Village

Eyam is another village steeped in history and interest. It is perhaps most well known because of the tenacity of its villagers when stricken by the plague in 1665. The story is well documented elsewhere but briefly, the disease reached the village in a consignment of cloth sent from London. Encouraged by their vicar, the villagers decided to cut themselves off from the outside world and although the disease abated during the cold winter months it returned with ferocious consequences in the summer of 1666. In all a total of 257 villagers died. Today, the Plague Cottage where it all started, can be seen on the main road just west of the church. The grassy area to the left of the cottages is the site of the old village pond and the village stocks still survive in front of the hall, which dates from the seventeenth century.

In the churchyard are graves to the plague victims including Catherine Mompesson, the wife of the vicar. William Mompesson acted as leader, comforter and liaison officer with the outside world but was not spared the life of his wife. She lies buried near to the village cross. The Celtic cross should not be missed. Although not complete, it is a remarkable survivor, perhaps all the more striking because the cross head survives on top of the shaft together with its intricate carving. Beyond the church one can find graves of plague victims who were buried in makeshift graves, perhaps to maintain family isolation, or when the graveyard reached its capacity. It makes one wonder how many lie in unmarked resting places beyond the churchyard wall. Look for the Hancock graves east of the village and the Talbot family graves in the family orchard at Riley House Farm, but please ensure that you do not trespass. Church services were held in the open during the time of the plague at **Cucklet Delf** and a service of remembrance is held there annually.

One of the main aspects of village life has been the local lead mining industry. The exploitation of lead ore, once paramount, is now secondary to fluorspar, which was once regarded as waste. Although Eyam Edge looks peaceful now and at first glance shows little sign of lead mining activities, this is very deceptive. The area has seen intense working over three centuries and even after most of the mines closed many of the tips were reworked for their fluorspar content.

Today Eyam is a small and attractive village nestling under Eyam Edge. It has several interesting streets with some fine properties and an attractive hall near to the church, completed in 1676 and now open to the public. On the hillside above the village sits Beech Hurst, an attractive house now converted into a youth hostel. Eyam Edge affords some good panoramic views marred perhaps by the fluorspar treatment plant of Laporte Industries at Cavendish Mill situated across Middleton Dale. It is nonetheless a salutary reminder that these beautiful places also have to sustain work to maintain the fabric of the area, whether we like the consequences of this or not. It comes as no surprise that from time to time the planning authority comes into conflict with industry; quarrying and mining operations present a continual problem in this conservation-conscious era. Laporte Industries process a very fine quality fluorspar from Sallet Hole Mine on Longstone Edge and from opencast workings, plus spar from other 'tributors' in the area.

Behind Eyam village, the ground rises to **Eyam Moor**, with its numerous cairns and stone circle. This high ground stretches northwards towards the Hope and Derwent Valleys and westwards to Great Hucklow where it is known as Abney Moor. The Bretton Brook cuts a big slice out of the moor and it drains the area to the north-west. The whole area is like a huge island, of about 10sq miles in extent, surrounded by edges and steeply descending ground. It is an area often neglected by tourists, yet the Great Hucklow to Hathersage road cuts right across the area. There are some good views across Eyam Moor from the road which runs past the gliding club at Camphill Farm, through the tiny village of **Abney** and also past

WALKS AROUND ABNEY AND EYAM MOOR

This moorland area has some good footpaths which enable you to explore it even better. A good circular route of about 10 miles gives a good impression of the area. Foolow makes a convenient starting point. It is a small but interesting village complete with its village green, pond and cross. Look out for the seventeenth-century hall and the manor house. The cross was possibly a boundary marker of the Royal Forest of the Peak. Take the Bretton road out of the village for about half a mile and then take the path to Abney Grange, first ascending Eyam Edge. Descend into Bretton Clough to cross the Bretton Brook and climb up to Abney Grange. Turn west at the grange and upon reaching the Hucklow Edge to Abney road, cross the road and Abney Moor to the junction of two lanes near Robin Hood's Cross of which only the base remains. It is probably a boundary cross, although it is also at the crossing of packhorse routes from Brough and Bradwell. At the junction bear right and proceed north-east along Shatton Lane around Shatton Edge. Descend some distance towards Shatton village before taking a path off to the right which leads roughly eastwards towards Offerton Hall. It nestles under Offerton Moor overlooking Hathersage with a fine view towards the moors which separate the Derwent Valley from Sheffield.

From Offerton Hall take the track to Highlow Hall rounding Offerton Moor and dropping down into the wooded Dunge Brook. Nearby is Robin Hood's Stoop (possibly a further cross base) from where (legend has it) he fired an arrow into Hathersage churchyard; a remarkable feat as the church is 1½ miles away! From here take the Abney road and opposite the drive to The Oaks drop down into the valley of Highlow Brook to Stoke Ford.

Here Abney Clough meets Bretton Clough and the path crosses a footbridge and climbs up the east side of Bretton Clough. A well defined track crosses Eyam Moor heading for Mag Clough where it reaches the road across Sir William Hill from Great Hucklow to Grindleford. Take the Eyam road which passes Mompesson's Well, named after William Mompesson, the rector of Eyam during the plague of 1665-6. At this time the village cut itself off from the

Highlow Hall. The latter is not a contradiction in terms in the Peak, for 'low' is a very common Derbyshire word meaning 'burial mound' or 'burial hill'. The hall was the home of the Eyre family and

outside world to contain the disease and arranged for food to be left at certain points around the village. This is one of the places.

There is also a barn near here just through a gate on the left. It is the former engine house to New Engine Mine; reputed to be the deepest lead mine shaft in Derbyshire at over 1,000ft deep. Unfortunately, the chimney became dangerous and was demolished. Pass the youth hostel at Beech Hurst and descend the road into the village. From Eyam, there is a choice of routes back to Foolow. Either take the road or the path through the fields just to the south of the road which is more pleasant and slightly more direct. If the climb out of Foolow, up the side of Eyam Edge, is too strenuous, start from the top of Eyam Edge and ignore Eyam village by turning right upon reaching the road across Sir William Hill.

A natural rock basin on Eyam Moor

is one of several sixteenth-century houses in the area. Offerton Hall to the north-west and Hazlebadge Hall south of Bradwell are other examples.

Castleton and its Caves

There is much to commend **Castleton** and it is easy to spend a day in the area. Even in poor weather, it is possible to avoid the rain by going underground in one of the four show caves or visiting the various shops, the church, information centre and museum (the Ollerenshaw Collection) in the village. Let us start however with the caves. Only one is a true cave — Peak Cavern, which is owned by the Duchy of Lancaster. It used to be known as the 'Devil's Arse in the Peak' but such vulgarity did not survive Victorian sensitivity. The cave system is very extensive, far more so than the portion open to the visitor. From its mouth flows the Peakshole Water, which originates as a number of streams flowing off the moor above. The cave entrance was, until the last ropemaker died a few years ago, used for making ropes and the rope walk can still be seen. Gone, however, are the little ropemakers' cottages which used to stand within the entrance to the cave itself. Ropes have been made here for centuries and Castleton brides used to be presented with a locally-made washing line.

Three more show caves, or more strictly speaking mines with natural caves in them, exist at Treak Cliff below Mam Tor. On Treak Cliff itself, are Blue John Mine and Treak Cliff Cavern. The former is a mine for Blue John stone, much favoured by the Victorians for decoration. The purplish stone is a variety of fluorspar that has been impregnated with hydrocarbons. The main veins, now fully exploited, were used to create beautiful vases and inlay work. Chatsworth has one of the largest vases turned from a single piece of stone and Kedleston Hall near to Derby has much Blue John inlay work. There is a good display of the stone, both in turned work and in cross sections, in Buxton Museum. Nowadays only a few hundredweights a year are mined, for costume jewellery. The age of the workings is unknown but it is unlikely to be more than two to three hundred years. Anything older is sheer speculation. Pompeii revealed vases in stone similar to Blue John but it has now been proved that this stone came from the Middle East not Castleton.

Blue John Mine descends steeply with countless steps to the bottom, which can be slippery in wet weather so ensure you wear suitable footwear. Treak Cliff Cavern includes some rather fine grottoes of stalactites and stalagmites which were discovered during a search for fresh veins of Blue John stone in 1926. The Speedwell Mine, actually across the Winnats Pass from Treak Cliff, is advertised as being a unique experience — the only mine where visitors are

CASTLETON'S CAVES

There are several caves around Castleton open to the public:

Blue John Cavern, Mam Tor. Old mine-workings for Blue John stone. The largest range of caverns containing veins of the stone.

Treak Cliff Cavern. Part natural and part an old mine for Blue John stone. Contains some attractive stalactites and stalagmites.

Speedwell Cavern, Winnats Pass. An old lead mine where visitors travel by boat on an underground canal.

Peak Cavern, Castleton village. A large cave system of which part is open to the public. The entrance was formerly used for the manufacture of ropes, and the ropewalk still survives.

Bagshawe Cavern, Bradwell. A show cave with an adventure trip, the latter by appointment only.

Odin Lead Mine. Although not a show cave (it must definitely **not** be entered by the public as it is very dangerous) it is the Peak District's oldest recorded lead mine and was one of the richest. There are the remains of a crushing mill just below the road beneath Mam Tor.

conducted underground by boat. The mine was designed like this in 1774. The man behind the scheme was John Gilbert, the agent to the Duke of Bridgewater and the man who introduced the duke to James Brindley. The Bridgewater Canal actually went underground to a boat-loading wharf near the coal face at Worsley near Manchester. John Gilbert was a partner in a copper mine at Ecton adjacent to the Duke of Devonshire's famous Ecton Mine and an underground canal was introduced at Ecton in 1767. Unfortunately the Speedwell Mine was uneconomic, in contrast to the Ecton and Worsley mines, and soon closed.

The adjacent **Winnats Pass** is spectacular. It is thought to have been eroded when it was under the sea rather than have been a former cave system. It is closed to heavy traffic but whether on foot, car or bike it is worth seeing. It used to be the main turnpike road until the latter was re-routed under Mam Tor because the gradient was easier. Unfortunately the face of **Mam Tor** is continually eroding due to hard bands of gritstone lying on softer shale. This has given rise to the name 'Shivering Mountain' but sometimes the movement is more severe, resulting in landslips that affect the road, causing

The keep of Peveril Castle perched over the entrance to Peak Cavern

The crushing circle at Odin Mine, Castleton

Mam Tor

subsidence on a large scale. The road is now permanently closed and has been abandoned completely. Meanwhile cars can use the Winnats Pass road, but should negotiate it with care, especially when it is icy. Heavy traffic must divert via Bradwell and Peak Forest.

Under Treak Cliff is the Odin Mine, which was worked for lead and not Blue John. Although its name implies a Saxon connection, there is no evidence of it being worked prior to the seventeenth century. Its main interest to the visitor is the crushing circle which survives on the east side of the road just above the Treak Cliff Cavern. The main entrance to the mine was lost during road-widening operations and although the large opening west of the road does lead into the workings these are dangerous and should not be entered. The crushing circle consists of a cast-iron track upon which lead ore would be heaped. This was then crushed by the millstone (of 5ft 10in diameter) which would be rolled around a pivot by a horse. The millstone with its circular iron tyre also survives, and it is an interesting relic of this bygone era and industry. The old mine tips are also a useful place to get out of the car and photograph the upper end of the Hope Valley and Castleton village itself.

If you do not feel energetic enough to visit the caves you can see the products of Blue John in the village gift shops and also visit the Ollerenshaw Collection of Blue John wares. The information centre has a display on lead mining, while a few yards away are the old hall (now a youth hostel) and the church, noted for its collection of old books which included, before it was stolen, a 1593 Cranmer Bible and a Breeches Bible.

The Castleton garland ceremony attracts a lot of interest on the evening of 29 May. The Garland King and his lady proceed on horseback through the village. The king carries a 60lb frame around him which is bedecked with flowers. The procession stops at each of the six inns in the village and eventually the garland is hoisted to hang from one of the pinnacles of the church tower, after the top bunch of flowers has been formally placed on the war memorial. It is pleasant to witness such ancient ceremonies surviving in our modern age.

Bradwell to Edale

Before leaving this area for the Edale Valley one must not forget **Bradwell**, nestling at the north end of Bradwell Dale. It grew as a mining community and it retains that character. It used to be famous for the hard hats made there which the miners used and which were known as 'Bradder Beavers'.

There are few 'attractions' here for the tourist except for Bagshawe
Cavern. The cave is reached by descending a flight of ninety-eight steps through an old lead mine. The show cave is half a mile in length past beautiful formations and other items of interest. Also a more adventurous caving trip is available. Mention has been made that old caves and mines should only be entered with an experienced guide. Here is one of the best with a guide included for a reasonable fee. This introduction to caving involves chimney climbing, ladderwork and crawling. The adventure trip, as it is known, needs to be booked in advance and you have to take at least a hand torch, strong shoes and old clothes. The address is given in the Additional Information.

Nearby is **Hope**. Its ancient church has a fourteenth-century
broach-spire which is unusual in the Peak District. The rest of the church is much later, but there are one or two interesting features such as a Saxon cross shaft in the churchyard and two fonts, one of the twelfth century and another of 1662 which was brought from Derwent church when the latter was demolished to make way for Ladybower Reservoir. Dominating the landscape behind the village are the twin hills of Lose Hill and Win Hill. Between the two hills
flows the River Noe to join the Peakshole Water at Hope village. This narrow valley carries the river together with the road and railway line to Edale. After 2 or 3 miles the valley turns westwards and opens out considerably. Here is the Vale of Edale in which the tiny village of Edale nestles under Kinder Scout. The peacefulness of this little valley is often ruptured in summer, but the tranquillity often returns in winter, particularly under a blanket of snow.

To the south of the valley is the ridge that runs from Lose Hill via Mam Tor to Lords Seat on Rushup Edge. Along the ridge runs a footpath which is an old packhorse route running from Chapel-en-le-Frith via Mam Tor and Hollins Cross to Hope and onwards through Hathersage to Sheffield. Today this is a marvellous footpath
which can be used as part of a 7 mile circular route based on Castleton. From the Market Place in Castleton, take the path up Cave Dale to where it reaches an old green lane between Dirtlow Rake and Eldon Hill. Bear north-west along the old Portway which heads for Mam Tor hillfort. From here take the ridge towards Lose Hill passing Hollins Cross and Back Tor; return to Castleton via the public right of way that runs from Lose Hill Farm via Riding House Farm and skirts the western side of Losehill Hall. Several old packhorse routes, now footpaths, meet at Hollins Cross. Indeed, it used to be the main road between Castleton and Edale and stories are still recalled of mill

*Edale church with
Kinder Scout behind*

*The ridge path from
Mam Tor towards
Lose Hill makes a
splendid walk*

The Vale of Edale

girls working in Edale who used to live in Castleton and walked this way to work, often having to spend the night at the mill when inclement weather prevented their return in the winter.

Losehill Hall is now a residential centre run by the National Park. From here are organised weekly courses covering many aspects of activities in the Peak District. Whether your interest is history, botany, geology, the history of old mines, caves, railways, or industrial archaeology of the area, all these interests and many more are catered for here.

A look on the map at the ground south of Rushup Edge shows various small streams which flow off the edge and suddenly disappear. These streams flow into a complex of underground passages which include Giant's Hole and the very wet cave well known in caving circles as P8, and reappears in Peak Cavern and the other

caves at Castleton. Giant's Hole lives up to its name for it is almost 500ft deep and a large system of passages leads out from its base. Just

to the south of Giant's Hole is Eldon Hole where the main entrance shaft is almost 200ft deep. Needless to say there are many other smaller cave systems and this particular area is very popular with cavers. Unfortunately many of the caves are watercourses and occasional cave rescue operations have to be mounted here.

Edale is not a very big village but it attracts thousands of visitors both during the summer months and in the winter when it is popular

with skiers. It also marks the beginning of the Pennine Way and many ramblers can be seen climbing the path up Grindsbrook. This is a delightful path with many interesting views back towards the village and over to Hollins Cross and Back Tor. The path leads up onto Kinder Scout and it is amazing just how many people head for this area ill prepared: for example, women in high-heeled shoes and other people with inadequate footwear or without waterproof clothing, etc. It needs to be clearly understood that Kinder Scout, Bleaklow and Saddleworth Moor beyond should not be treated lightly even in the summer. To put it bluntly, even in the summer these moors can be killers. This is not a case of trying to be melodramatic but simply stating facts. What can be a sunny pleasant day down in the valleys can turn into a nightmare with the descent of thick fog and mist up on the open moors and peat hags. Nonetheless for a well prepared rambler they offer wide open spaces with freedom of access virtually throughout the year. The only real problem to movement are the peat hags which give the impression of walking on a mattress, and the walker is continually climbing up over the top of a peat hag, only to drop down sometimes as much as 10ft to a little stream and then to

ACCESS LAND IN THE NATIONAL PARK

In the 1930s there was much pressure to allow free access to large areas of moorland contrary to the wishes of the landowners. This culminated in a mass trespass in 1932, when several hundred people left Hayfield village to climb up on to Kinder Scout. Despite the fact that the leaders were jailed after a show trial in Derby (one might even go so far as to say a staged trial) this was only the beginning. It was followed by other mass trespasses, political intrigue, double dealing and eventually the 1949 Act which paved the way for the access agreements which now exist.

The Peak District National Park was founded as a result of the *National Parks and Access to the Countryside Act* of 1949, which gave the National Park the authority to negotiate agreements with local landowners to permit access to open moorland, irrespective of whether rights of way across the land exist or not.

Access to the moors only exists where a right of way crosses the boundary of land classified as open land. The 'Dark Peak' OS Map shows the boundary of open land and the points of access, but does not cover the eastern moors. On access land one can wander freely, apart from on certain days in the grouse shooting season, between 12 August and 10 December, when parts of the moors are closed. Notices are placed in villages, on railway stations and at access points around the moors giving details, or they are available from the National Park at Aldern House, Bakewell.

There are currently 80 square miles of access land available for public use, most of it in the north of the Peak District National Park, but some also on the eastern moors. The public can wander at will on access land, although no damage must be done and it is recommended that you keep to obvious paths, both for your own safety and to avoid unnecessary erosion.

Bear in mind that on the large expanses of moor, such as Kinder Scout and Bleaklow, it is easy to become lost, especially if the mist comes down. It is wise to keep to one of the obvious paths that have been created by the passing of many feet, unless the weather is fine and you have a map and compass.

climb up to the top of the next hag, before dropping to the next stream, and so on. It is not without good reason that Edale has a mountain rescue post and information centre. There are also three National Trust Information Barns in the Edale Valley.

(opposite)
Kinder Downfall

*(right) Edale Cross,
situated on a medieval
road between Hayfield
and Edale*

*Kinder Reservoir and
William Clough*

Kinder Scout and Bleaklow

For those wishing to see the northern moors in a less strenuous manner there are two roads which cut through them. The northern one is the A628, the Woodhead road which heads towards Crowden from the Flouch Inn. On the western side of the watershed the valley becomes a long series of reservoirs built for Manchester Corporation. At the top is the oldest, Woodhead, followed by Torside, Rhodeswood, Valehouse and lastly Bottoms Reservoir, almost on the outskirts of Tintwistle village. Longdendale has recently seen an interesting development following the closure of the former main railway line between Sheffield and Manchester, which is now routed via Edale. The old track has been converted into a footpath called the Longdendale Trail, which, in turn, has been incorporated into the Pennine Trail. By using the trail and adjacent access land it is possible to plan excursions up onto the northern side of Kinder Scout or onto Bleaklow. However the reservoirs restrict the number of places where the valley may be crossed to reach Bleaklow. These valleys are wonderful areas to walk in good weather for those properly equipped — but not by inexperienced walkers, especially in misty conditions, when low cloud can disorientate you very quickly.

The more southerly route is the A57 road from Glossop to Sheffield. It is more commonly known as the Snake Road and both this and the Woodhead road feature regularly in winter road bulletins as the announcer advises listeners that the roads are blocked by snow. Part of this road is the old Roman road from Brough to Glossop, and as earlier indicated in this chapter, parts of the old road can be seen on Doctor's Gate just to the north of this road, on Coldharbour Moor. Today's traveller can, however, obtain better comfort than his predecessors because the Duke of Devonshire built an inn, now known as the Snake Pass Inn, in Ladyclough. If you do feel like doing a short walk without experiencing the rigours of the open moors why not take the footpath up Alport Dale to have a look at Alport Castles. This is not some medieval fortification but a natural outcrop in front of which is a large isolated mass of rock which became separated from the outcrop as a result of a landslip. Alport Castles are situated to the east of Alport Castles Farm which is about a mile up the dale from the main road at Alport Bridge.

Further up the A57 and beyond the Snake Pass Inn a bend in the road has been bypassed, making a small car park. If you park here and cross the road to enter the wood, a path drops to the river and follows it for a short distance downstream to where the river reaches a confluence with the stream emerging from Ashop Clough. There is a footbridge here which gives access to the path up the clough. This is a lovely walk and it can be used, like the path up to Alport Castles mentioned above, as a suitable route up onto the moors.

To the west of the moors lie the small towns of Glossop and Hayfield which are joined by the A624. To the west of this road rises Coombes Edge, which marks the western boundary of the Peak District at this point. The boundary of the Peak Park skirts around the towns of Hayfield and Glossop, which developed as textile towns in the nineteenth century. **Glossop** is the larger of the two and has some interesting old buildings particularly around the town centre and in old Glossop to the east of the town. **Hayfield**, however, is a useful starting point for walking up on to the western edge of Kinder Scout and in particular for a walk to Kinder Downfall. The Downfall is a waterfall where the River Kinder flows off the edge of Kinder Scout. It is particularly well known for blowing back with the force of the wind, and quite often it freezes up during the harshness of the winter months. South of Kinder Downfall is Edale Cross sitting on a medieval packhorse road from Hayfield via Jacobs Ladder to Edale. Below Kinder Reservoir is Kinder Quarry (now a car park) where the mass trespassers gathered in 1932. A plaque commemorates the event. Nearby is Bowden Bridge, an ancient packhorse bridge, built without side-walls as these interfered with the horses' panniers.

There is also a large area of the Peak District which exists to the north of Longdendale. While much of it consists of moorland there are many interesting and picturesque valleys which await exploration. Unfortunately the area is also well served by reservoirs as a quick look at the ordnance map reveals. It is an area certainly well worth discovering by car and there are plenty of opportunities for including a short walk in your itinerary. For example if one parks in Holme village a footpath leads northwards towards Digley Reservoir and crosses the water at its western end. The path climbs up to an old track and then one can walk above the northern shore of the reservoir towards the National Park car park at Digley Quarry. The road may then be taken over the dam and back to Holme. As you walk up the road towards the village look carefully at the capstones on the wall on your left. There are several lots of twin holes in the stones. These originally held tenter hooks and were used for drying cloth. South-west of Holmfirth and conspicuous for miles, is a modern windmill used for generating electricity at a local dairy. If you are a consumer of Longley Farm dairy products including yoghurt, this is where they are manufactured.

The drystone walls, in both the Dark Peak and the White Peak, need regular repair

Bowden Bridge, a packhorse bridge over the River Kinder near Hayfield

A quiet corner in Hayfield village

WALKS AROUND EDALE, KINDER SCOUT & BLEAKLOW

In view of the fact that you can exercise your own preference on the moors, certain routes are suggested in brief outline. These are perhaps the more interesting of the routes which cross the moors. It must be stressed again that the moors should not be crossed without adequate clothing, boots, food and with a compass and map. Also advise someone of your plans before setting out.

Hayfield, Kinder Downfall, Edale Cross (10 miles)

From Hayfield, take the road to Kinder Reservoir and then take the path up the northern side of the reservoir along White Brow. Proceed towards William Clough crossing the brook at the footbridge and traverse the rising ground to Kinder Downfall. This can be a trying walk which can be avoided by taking the longer route to the cairn at the head of William Clough and walking down the edge of Kinder Scout along the Pennine Way to Kinder Downfall. Return via Edale Cross and Tunstead Clough Farm.

Edale, Grindsbrook Clough (9 miles)

From the car park just before Edale village, close to the railway station, walk up the road through the village towards Grindsbrook and Kinder Scout. Cross the brook on a logbridge and walk up the valley eventually leaving the pasture. Gradually Edale Valley disappears from view and the path hugs the brook up onto the Kinder plateau. Follow the Pennine Way to Kinder Downfall. Return via Edale Cross and Jacob's Ladder to Upper Booth and then across fields to Edale. The views from Upper Grindsbrook and on the descent from Jacob's Ladder are particularly memorable.

Alport Bridge, Howden Reservoir, Hagg Farm (8 miles)

From Alport Bridge, just upstream from Hagg Farm on the A57 west of Ladybower Reservoir, take the track up to Alport Farm. Skirt the farm buildings and cross the brook before climbing up onto Birchinlee Pasture. The path follows Alport Castles Edge giving good views down Alport Dale and over to Kinder Scout. Take the path across Birchinlee Pasture and drop down the ridge above Ditch Clough into the wood. Walk along the road around to Howden Dam and on to Ouzelden Clough. From here a path climbs up out of the wood. It then follows the top of Gores Plantation, heading for Lockerbrook Farm and Hagg Farm. Alport Bridge lies 1½ miles up the road.

There is a network of youth hostels which enable the northern moors to be crossed with the knowledge that a bed (booked in advance) is ahead. The walks described below, *viz*: Crowden to Edale; Edale to Langsett; and Langsett to Crowden are outlined as individual daily walks although it is possible to do the round trip of Crowden-Edale-Langsett-Crowden in a day. It is not recommended unless you are an experienced long distance walker, however.

Crowden to Edale (16 miles)

From the youth hostel at Crowden, walk around to the dam of Woodhead Reservoir and walk down the B6015 to almost opposite the hostel. Walk under the bridge carrying the former railway and strike up the hill between Rollick Stones and Fair Vage Clough. Work around to Wildboarclough and follow this up to the top and on to Shining Clough Moss. Make for Far Moss and the Wain Stones on Bleaklow Head. From here, take the Pennine Way and follow this via Alport Low, across the Snake road and over Featherbed Moss to Mill Hill. Here the route turns south-east heading for Kinder Downfall. Cross Kinder Scout and Edale Moor before dropping down Grindsbrook into Edale.

The route described above from the B6015 to Shining Clough Moss is not recommended other than for very fit walkers. An easier route is to walk around the reservoir from Crowden Youth Hostel via Torside dam and follow the Pennine Way up Clough Edge via Torside Castle to Bleaklow Head.

Edale to Langsett (14½ miles)

From Edale a path skirts Kinder Scout and runs from Clough Farm to Jaggers Clough, through the wood above the ruined Elim Pits Farm to Haggwater Bridge and on to Hagg Farm. From Hagg Farm take the path via Lockerbrook Farm to Derwent Reservoir. Follow the road that follows the valley up past Derwent village and Howden reservoirs to Slippery Stones, where the Derwent village packhorse bridge was re-erected. Cross the bridge and take the path up Cut Gate on to Howden Edge. The path cuts across the moor to Mickleden Beck, dropping down towards Langsett. Cross Hingcliff Common to Brook House Bridge, climb the hill from the bridge to the top of the rise and turn right on the path through the woods to come into Langsett opposite the youth hostel.

Langsett to Crowden (10½ miles)

Take the path opposite the hostel drive heading into the wood and taking the path to Swinden Farm. Take the track from the farm known as Swinden Lane and head west before turning to the A628 and Milton Lodge. Walk along the road, again westwards to the Dog and Partridge Inn. Just beyond here take the old road which bears off to the right and eventually crosses the main road at Cabin Hill and heads for Lady Cross and Salters Brook. The latter is a reminder of the old days when packhorses loaded with salt passed this way heading for Sheffield. The old track crosses the main road once more and the defined track maintains its height above the River Etherow and the main road. Eventually Woodhead Reservoir is reached and the path drops down to the bridge over the spur of the reservoir. Follow the road for the last mile or so down to Crowden Youth Hostel. The hostel is open for non-members of the YHA.

Additional Information

Places to Visit

Bamford

Bamford Mill
SK205834
Cotton mill built about 1792 retaining its 30ft x 22ft wide waterwheel and a 1907 tandem-compound steam engine. Open days each year when the engine is run under steam. Visitors at other times by prior appointment.
☎ Hope Valley (0433) 651551.

Bradwell

Bagshawe Cavern
Jeffrey Lane
☎ Hope Valley (0433) 620540
Open: booked parties, caving or show cave, all year round. Adventure caving for novices; rugged show cave.

Castleton

Blue John Cavern and Blue John Mine
Buxton Road
☎ Hope Valley (0433) 620638/ 620642
Open: daily 9.30am-6pm (or dusk); closed 25-6 December & 1 January.
☎ 0443 620642.
World-famous source of Blue John stone and Castleton's greatest attraction for over 200 years. Of educational and geological interest. Free parking for cars and coaches.

Castleton Village Museum
Methodist Church Rooms
☎ (0433) 620483/620518
Open: Easter & Bank Holiday weekends; May, September & October, Sunday; June & July, Sunday & Wednesday; August, Tuesday-Thursday & Sunday. 2-5pm.

Ollerenshaw Collection
(The Cavendish House Museum)
Cross Street
☎ Hope Valley (0433) 620642
Open: daily, 9.30am-6pm (dusk in winter) except 25-6 December and 1 January.
Adjoining the original Blue John Stone Craft Shop. Private museum of Derbyshire treasures, including one of the largest and finest collections of Blue John stone.

Peak Cavern
☎ Hope Valley (0433) 620285
Open: Easter-end October, daily, 10am-5pm. Closed Mondays in low season.

Peveril Castle (English Heritage)
On the south side of Castleton
☎ (0433) 620613
Open: daily April-September 10am-6pm, October-March Tuesday-Sunday 10am-4pm. Closed 24-6 December, 1 January . Norman Castle founded in 1068. Steep climb, but magnificent views.

Speedwell Cavern
Winnats Pass
☎ Hope Valley (0433) 620512
Open: daily, 9.30am-5.30pm; closed 25-6 December & 1 January.
Boat trip along flooded mine level to natural cavern.

Treak Cliff Cavern
¾ mile west of Castleton on A625.
☎ Hope Valley (0433) 620571
Open: summer 9.30am-5.30pm, winter 9.30am-4pm; closed 25 Dec. Richest known visible veins of Blue John with fine displays of stalagmites and stalactites.

Chapel-en-le-Frith

Chestnut Centre
On the Castleton road (A625) near
Cheapel-en-le-Frith
☎ (0298) 814099
Conservation park, otter haven and
owl sanctuary, 40 acres of land-
scaped grounds.

Eyam

Eyam Hall
☎ (0433) 631976
Open: April-October Wednesday,
Thursday, Sunday & Bank Holiday
Monday 11am-4.30pm.
Guides tours, café and shop.

Glossop

Glossop Heritage Centre
Henry Street
☎ (0457) 869176
Open: Monday-Saturday 10.30am-
4.30pm
Development of the town over ten
thousand years of its history. Art
Gallery and craft area, permanent
and changing exhibitions.

New Mills

New Mills Heritage Centre
Rock Mill Lane
☎ (0663) 746904
Open: Tuesday-Friday 11am-4pm,
Saturday & Sunday 10.30am-
4.30pm. Closed Monday, except
Bank Holiday Mondays.

Tourist Information Centres

Castleton (National Park)
Castle Street
☎ Hope Valley (0433) 620679

Edale (National Park)
Fieldhead
☎ Hope Valley (0433) 670207

Glossop
The Gate House, Victoria Street
☎ Glossop (0457) 855920

Holmefirth
49-51 Huddersfield Road
☎ 0484 687603

6
THE DERWENT VALLEY
& THE GRITSTONE EDGES

The valley of the River Derwent is one of the most pronounced features of the Peak District landscape. The river draws its water initially from the sodden peat hags of Featherbed Moss, where a fan of little streams collect to flow south-east before turning to run in the southerly direction which characterises much of its length through the Peak. The valley soon becomes deeply entrenched, with green fields rising steeply towards the moors. A feature down the length of the valley as far as Chatsworth is the escarpment of gritstone rocks which outcrop on its eastern side. Their total length is around 20 miles and most can be followed on foot. From the valley these edges dominate the skyline. Now they offer sport to climbers, vantage points to visitors and an interesting linear path for ramblers.

The Derwent is the major river of the region. In ancient times it must have been a formidable obstacle when in flood. There is a pattern of packhorse routes and salt ways crossing the Peak, heading for Sheffield, Chesterfield and places to the east, all having to descend to and cross the Derwent. Bridges were built at an early date; the existing bridge at Baslow was built before 1500, while the predecessor of the bridge upstream at Calver was also recorded in the fifteenth century. Derwent village bridge, now re-erected at Slippery Stones, was built in the Middle Ages and it is recorded that it was repaired in 1682. Downstream, a bridge is recorded at York-shire Bridge in 1599 when a wooden structure was rebuilt in stone.

The construction of the Derwent reservoirs has had a significant impact on the upper part of the valley, flooding also the Woodlands Valley which climbs up the moors towards the Snake Pass and Glossop. The Howden and Derwent dams were built together, work starting on the former in 1901 and the latter a year later. Howden was

149

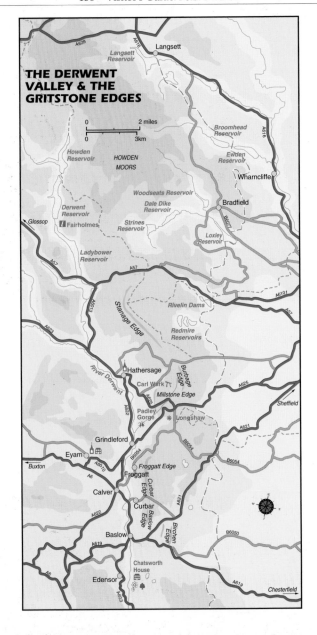

THE DERWENT
VALLEY & THE
GRITSTONE EDGES

Pony trekking near Hope Cross, above the Ladybower Reservoir

Ladybower Reservoir

finished in 1912 but Derwent took until 1916 to complete. A temporary village was built for the navvies building the dams. It was known as Birchinlee and was situated by the present road halfway up the west side of Howden Reservoir. The population rose to over 900 people and it had a shop, hospital, village hall, school and chapel.

Derwent and Ashopton villages were inundated by the rising waters of the Ladybower Reservoir. The remains of Ashopton are now covered by layers of silt, but in times of exceptional drought the outline of Derwent village may be seen again. Even the stumps of trees cut down in the 1940s reappear, creating the outline of the original fields.

Derwent Dam found a new use during World War II for it was used by RAF 617 squadron for practice runs before the dambusters raid on Germany and again in the film of the raid. From time to time the RAF pays tribute with a flypast by a Lancaster bomber. Unfortunately such events — including the drought conditions — attract enormous crowds and the roads are choked with traffic.

Between the wars, Derwent Hall was used as a youth hostel and was opened by the Prince of Wales in 1932. It was built in 1672 by the Balguy family but was demolished in 1943, along with Derwent church and village. The church spire was left standing for a few years and the east window was moved to Hathersage Church. The packhorse bridge was placed in store in 1938 and rebuilt in 1959 upstream at Slippery Stones. Ladybower Reservoir, which flooded both Derwent and Ashopton villages, was opened in 1945 by King George VI, having taken ten years to complete, and at the time it was the largest man-made lake in the country. Derwent village was situated roughly where the Mill Brook would have reached the River Derwent, and Ashopton village was immediately adjacent to Ashopton viaduct and on its south side. It is interesting that even the 1976 'Dark Peak' tourist map still showed Derwent church tower surrounded by water at SK185886, even though it was demolished in 1947. An interesting series of photographs showing the villages and Birchinlee appear in *Bygone Days in the Peak District*.

Man's use of the river and its valley does, of course, go back further. Its water was used to power mills, levels from mines were driven to drain them to the river and quarries have hewn stone for roads, walls, dam construction and millstones. Hundreds of unsold millstones litter the quarries of the eastern edge. Many can be seen at Millstone Edge on the A625 south-east of Hathersage at SK249799. They lie either side of an old track to Bole Hill Quarry which was reworked to supply stone to Ladybower dam.

Despite the urbanisation of parts of the valley, there is still much to see which will interest the visitor. The reservoirs have a beauty of their own, and the dams are particularly impressive when overflowing, especially the Derwent Dam. Unfortunately the woods which surround the upper two reservoirs add little harmony to the scene, for they are stark and emphasise a heavy shoreline, particularly when the water level drops. Nonetheless, the road from Ashopton viaduct is worth taking to the top of Howden Reservoir. It finishes at a cul-de-sac where there is a path which leads the short distance to Slippery Stones where the Derwent village packhorse bridge was rebuilt in 1959.

On Sundays and Bank Holiday Mondays between Easter and the end of October, visitors must park at Fairholme, near Derwent Dam (except cars displaying a disabled person's orange disc). To get further up the valley, you must walk, hire a bike or catch the regular minibus service to the Kings Tree.

Hiring a bike at Fairholme at the southern end of Derwent Reservoir and cycling round the reservoirs is a good way of exploring the area. A suggested route is to go up the valley from Fairholme on the western side of Derwent Reservoir and on around Howden Reservoir. Return down the eastern side of the valley as far as the Sheffield-Glossop road at the Ashopton viaduct. Cross this and return up the road to Fairholme. This last section is used by motor vehicles and so care should be exercised, although there is only limited traffic north of Fairholmes and very little on the eastern side of the valley.

Before moving on to the southern part of the valley, it is worth visiting the area to the northeast of the great reservoirs. The valleys here drain into the River Don and thence the Humber quite independently of the Derwent/Trent river system, but they have a character similar to the Upper Derwent Valley, many of them also with reservoirs, albeit on a smaller scale.

The area includes the Loxley and Ewden valleys where the moors are lower. Above the Loxley Valley and Strines Reservoir is Boot's Folly, a stone tower built to find work for unemployed men. Much of the moorland has been cultivated, used for plantations or inundated beneath reservoirs. It was here that the Dale Dike Reservoir, upstream of Low Bradfield, collapsed when it first filled in 1865. A total of 238 people were drowned and over 600 buildings were destroyed or damaged as the flood swept towards Sheffield.

Above Low Bradfield, with its village cricket pitch, is High Bradfield. Here there is a motte and bailey castle and an interesting church which retains its former watch house, built to deter body

Boot's Folly and Strines Reservoir

Strines Inn

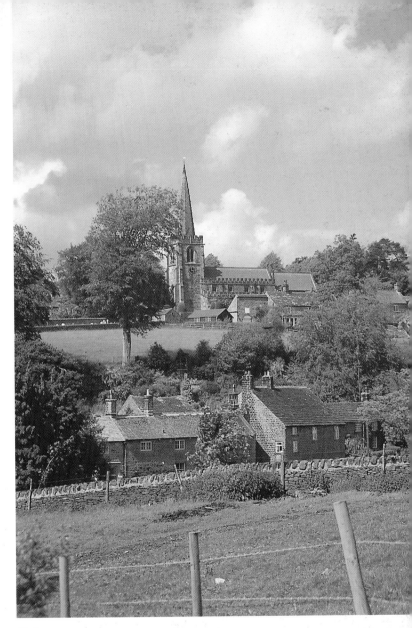

Hathersage

snatchers and now converted to a small dwelling. A trip around the area, including the ancient Strines Inn, Bolsterstone, Ewden and the Bradfield villages is recommended if you can follow the little lanes on a motoring map.

A little to the north of this area is the tiny village of Langsett, with the Langsett Barn National Park Visitor Centre on the A616 between Stocksbridge and Holmfirth. Housed in a restored seventeenth-century aisled barn, there are displays about the 120 acre Langsett Reservoir, completed in 1904. The valve tower on the dam has a castellated top and is a replica of a tower at Lancaster Castle!

The Lower Derwent & the Gritstone Edges

Some 4 miles southeast of Ladybower Reservoir is **Hathersage**. It has associations with Charlotte Brontë who wove her novel *Jane Eyre* around the area, calling the town Morton. In the churchyard is the gravestone of Little John, the friend and companion of Robin Hood. Apparently he was a native of Hathersage, was known as John Little, and made his living as a nailer until he found everlasting fame. The town has a passenger railway station on the line between Sheffield and Manchester which also has stations at Grindleford, Bamford, Hope and Edale.

Leaving Hathersage towards Sheffield the road climbs up to Millstone Edge. Just before the sharp bend with its viewpoint — approached from the opposite direction the valley suddenly opens up before you and you will appreciate why it is known as Surprise View — there is a National Trust sign on the right marked Bole Hill. A path runs down an old railway track into the wood where there are hundreds of abandoned millstones. Although this is the largest concentration, they can be found scattered along all the gritstone edges above the eastern side of the Derwent Valley. Millstones were sent from here to places as far away as Russia, but the trade suddenly collapsed in the nineteenth century with the introduction of new methods of grinding corn, and the already finished stones were abandoned. Some, shaped like a mushroom cap, are much older and it is not clear why these were abandoned.

South of the town the Burbage Brook flows through Padley Wood to join the Derwent at **Grindleford**. The descent of the brook through the wood is steep and the brook rushes amid boulders and trees in a steep sided valley. It is a beauty spot missed by many visitors who overlook it. It is best visited by walking upstream to get the best views of the rushing white water. The 3½ mile walk starts by a bus stop on the B6521, immediately above Grindleford Station, where a stile gives access to the wood. The path is easy to follow and upon passing through a gate, drops down a series of steps to a footbridge. Once over the brook, the path climbs steeply to an elevated level above the stream. Eventually the path leaves the wood and crosses through flat fields to reach the A625. Ahead lies Stanage Edge, and by the main road Toad's Mouth Rock, a curious natural rock formation overlooked by Carl Wark, a hillfort of the Iron Age. It has a huge platform built of gritstone blocks up to 5ft across and ramparts 10ft high. To the south is the Longshaw Estate, purchased from the Duke of Rutland by subscription and given to the National Trust when he sold his 11,500 acre estate here in 1927. A path returns to Grindleford through the estate, past the house and its lake. This is the site for the Longshaw Sheepdog Trial held every September. There is a National Trust Information Centre, shop and cafeteria at Longshaw.

Before leaving the Longshaw area the chapel at **Padley** should not be missed. This is reached by taking the unmade track beyond Grindleford Railway Station. It is the final remnant of Padley Hall. whose excavated foundations can be seen at the rear. The hall was built in the fourteenth and fifteenth centuries by the Catholic Fitzherbert family. Two priests were arrested here in 1588 and subsequently executed at Derby. The chapel fell into disuse, but was restored in 1933 after the discovery of the altar. A rememberance service for the 'Padley Martyrs' is held here annually on the Thursday nearest to 12 July.

The gritstone edges are a prominent geological feature east of the River Derwent. Outstanding examples are Birchen Edge, Gardom's Edge, Baslow Edge, Curbar Edge, Froggatt Edge, Millstone Edge, Burbage Edge and Stanage Edge. There are paths along the tops of most of these edges and all give spectacular views. Many are popular with rock climbers. On Birchen Edge is Nelson's Monument, erected in 1810 by a local man, while Baslow Edge has a monument to Wellington, erected in 1866. Near to Nelson's Monument are three huge rocks looking like ships with the names *Victory*, *Defiant*, and *Royal Soverin* [*sic*] on their bows. Most unusual in an area so far from the sea.

These edges offer the opportunity of a marvellous linear walk, from the signposted path by a stile on the Baslow side of the Robin Hood Inn on the A619 (SK277722). The path cuts around Gardom's Edge and then crosses the A621 heading for Wellington's Monument. From here it follows Baslow, Froggatt and Curbar Edges, passing a small stone circle by Froggatt Edge. The views along the

The grave in Hathersage churchyard, reputed to be that of Little John

Abandoned millstones stacked up in Bole Hill Quarry

The Iron Age hillfort of Carl Wark with Higger Tor behind

edges down into the Derwent Valley and across to Eyam Moor and Longstone Moor are marvellous. It is difficult to appreciate that the outskirts of Sheffield are only 4 to 5 miles away. A footpath to Nether Padley leads to Padley Gorge and the climb back towards Stanage Edge which winds around to Moscar above Bamford Moor and Ladybower Reservoir. However this walk ends 15 miles from the start, so another car or a helpful second driver are needed. Alternatively a series of separate walks along the individual edges may be planned.

In the valley bottom below below the gritstone edges lie the villages of Calver and Baslow. That part of **Calver**, by the traffic lights and known as Calver Sough, takes its name from an old lead mine, last worked in the mid-nineteenth century when a steam pumping engine was erected close to the crossroads. Just to the north of Calver is Stoke Hall. After being empty for some time, this beautiful building has been renovated. There is an attractive walk between the bridges at Froggatt and Calver. A path follows each side of the river and makes a good circular walk. It is easier to park near Calver Bridge than at Froggatt. The river is deep, wide and slow moving and the broad expanse of water looks very attractive on a sunny day. The former cotton mill at Calver was built by Richard Arkright in 1803-4 and was used to film the television series *Colditz*. Near the fine eighteenth-century stone bridge is a craft centre with a bookshop and cafeteria.

Above Calver's bridge, on the eastern side of the valley is the village of **Curbar**. Marked on the OS 'White Peak' map are the graves of the Cundy family, victims of the plague. They date from 1632 and five interments lie beneath rough-hewn slabs of limestone. Nearby and a little further down the hillside is an unusual building, square with a conical stone slab roof. It was used as a lock-up and then a dwelling until 1935. Although on private ground, a footpath in a nearby field comes close to it.

Baslow is divided into Over End, Nether End and Bridge End. At the latter there is an interesting medieval bridge with a very small guard house, just large enough for one person to collect tolls. The nearby church has an unusual clock with 'VICTORIA 1897' instead of numerals, while inside is a dog whip used to chase stray dogs out during church services.

Most visitors to Baslow are attracted to Nether End with its little shops set around a green. Beyond the impressive Cavendish Hotel, is a car park. If you prefer a 1½ mile walk to Chatsworth, rather than driving there, then park here. Cross the little brook a few yards eastwards from the car park and take the signposted path down the brookside past a rare sight in this area—a thatched cottage. The path crosses the river meadows and reaches Chatsworth by Queen Mary's Bower and the elegant bridge over the river.

Chatsworth, the home of the Cavendish family, is one of the Wonders of the Peak, and one of the finest houses in Britain. The son of William Cavendish and Bess of Hardwick was created first Earl of Devonshire, and his descendant, the fourth Earl, was created the first Duke of Devonshire for supporting the cause of William of Orange. Bess of Hardwick brought considerable wealth to the Cavendish family and with the dissolution of the monasteries, this wealth was used to purchase land on a large scale throughout the Peak District and elsewhere. The wealth from landed property was augmented, chiefly during the eighteenth century, by considerable royalties from lead mines in the Peak District and also from copper ores from the duke's mine at Ecton in the Manifold Valley. Between 1760 and 1817, the Ecton mine alone produced an estimated profit of £335,000, and this enormous income helped create a dynasty of extremely wealthy men. As a consequence, Chatsworth is a treasure house, richly endowed with old masters, priceless furniture, tapestries, carvings and porcelain.

Today it is open to visitors and the route taken through the house includes the majority of the main state rooms on the south front. Much of the present house was built by the first and sixth dukes, ie in the seventeenth century and in the early part of the nineteenth century. It therefore makes an interesting comparison with the older Haddon Hall. Perhaps one of the most fortunate aspects of Chatsworth is that a considerable number of its treasures are on display. Everywhere one goes in the house there are priceless and beautiful works of art. You should allow plenty of time for a walk around Chatsworth, for there is so much that otherwise will be missed. For instance, the wood and alabaster carvings in the chapel and the painting of the violin in the music room. At the end of the tour there is now a shop in the former orangery which leads out into the garden.

The 106 acre garden is also worthy of a visit. In fact, it should be given at least half a day of your time in order to explore the various points of interest. It includes the Emperor Fountain which is set in its canal pond and is noted for being the highest gravity fed fountain in the world, although seldom seen at its full height of 260ft. Elsewhere in the gardens is the maze, set on the site of what used to be the conservatory built by Paxton and a forerunner of his Crystal Palace

The restored chapel at Padley

The Eagle Stone above Baslow Edge

Stanage Edge

which was built in London for the Great Exhibition of 1851. Behind the house are the cascades and the aqueduct, together with Stand Wood with its various footpaths along the valley side. Above the wood stands the prospect tower, a relic of the Elizabethan manor house that existed here before the present house was built. A more recent innovation has been the development of a forestry and farming display plus an adventure playground, which is always a special treat for children. By the forestry exhibition is a ten-ton pile of timber, representing just 24 hour's growth on the estate's 2,500 acres of woodland. There are no lions and safari parks here, but there are several festivals at different times of the year, which can add immensely to a visit to this wonderful place.

If you like to ramble do not overlook Chatsworth Park. There are several private paths through the park to which the public are permitted access and these are shown on notice boards. If you are south of the house itself, look out for the deer on the east bank of the river. At the southern end of the park, close to One Arch Bridge (with traffic lights) is Carlton Lees picnic area and car park set amid the trees above the road. It is a useful place to park if exploring the estate paths and a notice board indicates the paths. There is a tea bar and the estate sells a leaflet about its Stand Wood walks which take you above and behind Chatsworth House.

In Stand Wood you can walk in comparative quietness around the lakes which supply water to the garden. Quite a long walk can be planned if you so wish. The path climbs up through the wood to the Hunting Lodge, built in the sixteenth century by Bess of Hardwick, the builder of Hardwick Hall and the previous house at Chatsworth which stood on the same site as the present building.

Close to Chatsworth is Edensor village, built in 1838-42 by Joseph Paxton to house the inhabitants of the original village. All the houses are of different styles and the church stands in a dominating situation above the houses. Here lies buried Kathleen Kennedy, the sister of the late US President. She was married to the Marquis of Hartington, the son of the 10th Duke of Devonshire. Just one house remains in the old Edensor village by the side of what was the main street, between the cattle grid and the drive to the house. Its owner held his own freehold and refused to sell to the duke.

If you like looking around country houses like Chatsworth, then *Visitor's Guide: Treasure Houses of England* is recommended. It describes Beaulieu, Blenheim Palace, Broadlands, Castle Howard, Chatsworth House, Warwick Castle and Woburn Abbey, and also recommends other attractions, accommodation and places to eat.

Additional Information

Places to Visit

Baslow

✳ *Chatsworth Estate Farm Shop*
Stud Farm, Pilsley
1 ½ miles from Chatsworth House
☎ Baslow (024688) 3392
Open: Monday-Saturday,
9am-5.30pm all year round.
Fine selection of fresh meats,
vegetables and ready prepared
foods, including game from the
estate in the season.

Chatsworth House
☎ Baslow (0246) 582204
Open: April-end October (dates
may vary a little), daily 11.30am-
4.30pm.
Historic house and garden.
Farming and forestry exhibition
and adventure playground, open
end March-end September,
10.30am-4.30pm.
There is a family admission to the
farmyard and adventure playground. For the price of two adults
and one child, up to three more
children go in free. No dogs (but
dog pound provided).

Craft Centres

Baslow

Derbyshire Craft Centre
Calver Bridge
☎ Hope Valley (0433) 631231
Open: daily, 10am-6pm, closed 25-6
December 1 January and 2nd two
weeks in January.
Largest craft shop in the county.
Eating house (Egon Ronay
recommended), playroom for
children, ample car parking.

Grindleford

Andrew Lawton Furniture
Goatscliffe Workshops
Immediately on the left on entering
Grindleford on B6001 from Calver.
☎ Hope Valley (0433) 631754
Open: Monday-Friday 9am-5pm,
Saturday 10am-5pm.
High quality furniture hand-made
to modern designs. Commissions
welcome. Pieces available for direct
sale in showroom.

Tourist Information Centres

Chesterfield

Information and Heritage Centre
Low Pavement
☎ Chesterfield (0249) 207777 / 8

Fairholmes (Peak Park)

Derwent Valley
Situated below Derwent Dam
☎ 0433) 650953
Open: Easter-October daily
10.30am-5.30pm approx; winter
Saturday & Sunday.

Langsett (National Park)

Near Penistone

Torside (National Park)

Longdendale
No telephone
Both open: Easter-September
Saturday, Sunday & Bank Holiday
Monday 10.30am-5pm approx.

Sheffield

Town Hall extension
Union Street
☎ Sheffield (0742) 734671

Baslow bridge

The Emperor fountain and the south front of Chatsworth House

Chatsworth House and
the River Derwent

Laburnum tunnel in
the gardens at
Chatsworth House

7
AROUND THE PEAK DISTRICT

The Peak District is a relatively small area and, given the right weather conditions, it would take more than one holiday in the National Park to visit all its various attractions. But if one is unfortunate enough to visit the Peak during a spell of wet weather, and have already visited the major indoor attractions detailed in the various chapters of this book, then you might wish to look slightly further afield. On all sides of the Peak District there are adventure parks, stately homes (some, such as Hardwick Hall and Kedleston Hall are of national importance), museums and steam railways which justify a visit. As this book takes a liberal view as to the definition of the Peak District it is not confined to the strict boundaries of the National Park, so some of these places, such as Alton Towers and the country houses on the Cheshire fringe, have been included in earlier chapters. Here are some other suggestions for places to visit.

Burton-on-Trent
Bass Museum of Brewing
Horninglow Street
☎ (0283) 42031

Cheshire
Jodrell Bank Science Centre and Tree Park
2 miles north of Holmes Chapel
☎ (0477) 71571
Open: daily throughout the season.
Planetarium, Lovell telescope, inter-active science gallery and 35 acre Tree Park.

Styal Country Park (National Trust)
Quarry Bank Mill
Styal, Cheshire
☎ (0625) 527468
A whole village owned by the National Trust includes a former water driven cotton mill dating from 1784, now a museum of the early days of the cotton industry. Quarry Bank Mill is claimed to be the best surviving Georgian cotton mill and Styal village the least altered industrial revolution factory colony.

Chesterfield

Bolsover Castle
6 miles east of Chesterfield
Open: daily, April to September,
Monday-Saturday 10am-6pm;
October to March, Tuesday-Sunday
10am-4pm. Seventeenth-century
mansion on the site of a twelfth-
century castle.

Chesterfield Museum
St Mary's Gate
☎ (0246) 559727
Open: Monday, Tuesday, Thurs-
day-Saturday 10am-4pm
Story of Chesterfield from Roman
times to present day. Medieval
builders' wheel, George
Stephenson memorabilia.

Hardwick Hall (National Trust)
Doe Lea
7 miles southeast of Chesterfield
☎ (0246) 850430
Open: April-mid-September only
on weekends, Wednesdays and
Thursdays plus Bank Holiday
Mondays, 1-5pm.
Magnificent Elizabethan mansion
built by Bess of Hardwick.

Derby

Calke Abbey (National Trust)
Ticknall, near Melbourne, 8 miles
south of Derby
☎ (0332) 864444 24-hour recorded
information
☎ (0332) 863822 general enquiries
Open: April-October Saturday-
Wednesday and Bank Holiday
Monday. House 1-5.30pm; garden
and church 11am-5.30pm; last
admission 5pm. Timed entry.
Park open during daylight hours
all year.
Baroque mansion, built 1701-3 and
unaltered since 1924. 'The house
that time forgot.'

Derby Industrial Museum
Silk Mill lane,
off Full Street
☎ (0332) 255308
Open: Monday 11am-5pm,
Tuesday-Saturday 10am-5pm,
Sunday and Bank Holidays 2-5pm.
Derbyshire industries, including
Rolls-Royce aero engines.

Derby Museum & Art Gallery
The Strand
☎ 0332 255586
Open: Monday 11am-5pm,
Tuesday-Saturday 10am-5pm,
Sunday and Bank Holidays 2-5pm.
Local history, archaeology, natural
history, Derbyshire clocks and
paintings by Joseph Wright.

*Elvaston Castle Working Estate
    Museum*
5 miles southeast of Derby.
☎ (0332) 571342
Open: April to October, Wednesday-Saturday 1-5pm, Sunday and
Bank Holidays 10am-6pm.
Recreates the past through displays
and demonstrations in and around
the original workshops and cottages.

Kedleston Hall (National Trust)
4 miles northwest of Derby
☎ (0332) 842191
Open: end March to end October,
Saturday-Wednesday 1-5.30pm
(last admissions to house 5pm).
Park and garden open 11am-6pm
on the same days.
Palladian mansion set in classical
park landscape. Most complete and
least altered sequence of Robert
Adam interiors in England. Indian
museum with objects collected by
Lord Curzon when Viceroy of
India (1899-1905); Adam bridge
and fishing pavilion in the park;
garden and pleasure grounds.

The Georgian cotton mill at Styal in Cheshire

Hardwick Hall 'more glass than wall' proudly displays the monogram of its builder, Elizabeth Shrewsbury

Calke Abbey, near Melbourne, south of Derby

The gardens and south front of Kedleston Hall

Pickford House Museum
41 Friar Gate
☎ 0332 255363
Open: Monday 11am-5pm,
Tuesday-Saturday 10am-5pm,
Sunday and Bank Holidays 2-5pm.
Restored Georgian town house
with period interiors and furniture.

Sudbury Hall (National Trust)
Sudbury
10 miles east of Derby on A50, 10
miles south of Ashbourne.
☎ (028 3585) 305
Open: early April to September,
Wednesday-Sunday plus Bank
Holiday Mondays, 1-5.30pm. Last
admission 5pm. Closed Good
Friday.
Charles II house with fine late
seventeenth-century decoration,
plus Museum of Childhood. Light
lunches and teas served in former
coach house.

Ilkeston

The American Adventure Theme Park
Just off the M1 at junction 26.
☎ (0773) 531521
Open: Easter week, May Bank
Holidays and weekends to end
May; June-September daily; partial
opening in September & October.
Wild West action and adventure
with a superb range of rides and
entertainments, free once entrance
fee has been paid.

Ripley

Midland Railway Steam Centre
Butterley Station
☎ (0773) 570140
Open: every weekend March to
December. Also during main
school holidays. Passenger trains
operate 11.15am-4.15pm on 3½
mile preserved railway. Museum

and animal farm with model
railway, plus narrow gauge and
miniature railway.

Sheffield
Abbeydale Industrial Hamlet
Abbeydale Road South (A621)
☎ (0742) 367731
Open: Tuesday-Saturday 10am-
5pm, Sunday 11am-5pm. Also
Bank Holiday Monday. Closed 25-6
December, 1 January.
Restored waterpowered eight-
eenth-century scythe and steel-
works, with four waterwheels, tilt
hammers, hand forges, workmen's
cottage and manager's house.
Occasional working days. Café.

Bishop's House

Meersbrook Park,
Norton Lees Lane
☎ (0742) 557701
Open: Wednesday-Saturday 10am-
4.30pm, Sunday 11am-4.30pm.
Open Bank Holiday Mondays,
closed 24-6 December & 1 January.
Earliest and best preserved
example of a timber-framed
building in the area. Also exhibitions and activities.

Sheffield City Museum
Weston Park
☎ (0742) 768588
Open: Monday-Saturday 10am-
5pm, Sunday 11am-5pm. Closed
Christmas.
Specialities are the craftsmanship
of cutlery and Old Sheffield Plate,
local archaeology, geology, wildlife, natural history and weather.

Sheffield Industrial Museum
Kelham Island
Off Alma Street
☎ (0742) 722106

Open: Wednesday-Saturday 10am-5pm, Sunday 11am-5pm. Open Bank Holiday Mondays, but closed 24-6 December.

The story of Sheffield's industrial evolution with displays, films and workshops. Rolling mill engine run on steam daily. Working craftsmen.

Shepherd Wheel
Whitely Woods
Hangwater Road
☎ (0742) 367731
Open: Wednesday-Saturday 10am-12.30pm and 1.30-5pm, Sunday 11am-12.30pm and 1.30-5pm. Closes 4pm in winter. Open Bank Holiday Mondays, but closed 24-6 December.

The story of Sheffield industry back to 1584. Waterwheel run regularly, water supply permitting.

Stoke-on-Trent

Ford Green Hall
Smallthorne
On the B5051, 2½ miles north of Hanley
☎ (0782) 534771
Open Sunday-Thursday 1-5pm. Guided tours at 1.15, 2.15, 3.15 and 4.15pm, taking 45 minutes. Free Timber-framed farmhouse built in 1624 with eighteenth-century additions, occupied by the Ford family until the end of the eighteenth century. Rooms furnished to show how they might have lived. Free parking.

Foxfield Light Railway
Caverswall Road
Blythe Bridge
☎ (0782) 396210
Open: every weekend throughout the year. Steam trains operate on

Sundays and Bank Holidays, Easter to September. Also wine and dine trains on most Saturday evenings in summer. Buffets available for private parties.
Three miles of track, museum with static locomotives, shop and buffet.

Gladstone Pottery Museum
Uttoxeter Road, Longton
☎ (0782) 319232 or 311378
Open: March to October, Monday-Saturday (including Bank Holidays) 10.00am-5.00pm, Sunday 2-5pm. Closed Mondays November to February. Last admission 1 hour before closing.
Unique Victorian pottery factory. Hands-on dispays, make your own flower in china clay. Shop. Teashop.

Wedgwood Visitor Centre   ☀
Barlaston
5 miles south of Stoke. Follow brown tourist signposts from A34 and M6.
☎ (0782) 204218 or 204141
Open: all year (except Christmas and New Year) including bank holidays, Monday-Friday 9am-5pm, Saturday 10am-4pm, summer Sundays 10am-4pm (Easter to October).
Facilities include a film show, shop, museum, art gallery and refreshments.

A full list of potteries open to the public is available from the Town Hall, Hanley, Stoke-on-Trent.

Other factories include Spode China
☎ (0782) 46011.

Hanley Museum contains one of the world's finest collections of ceramics.

Peak District: Fact File

Accommodation

Lists of various types of accommodation may be obtained from some information offices. Lists are prepared by the Peak District National Park and the district councils of Staffordshire Moorlands, Derbyshire Dales and High Peak. The tourist board guides may be confusing as North West, Yorkshire, Heart of England and East Midlands areas all cover different parts of the Peak.

Some addresses which can supply accommodation lists are:

Bakewell Tourist Information
  Office
Old Market Hall, Bridge Street
Bakewell
☎ (0629) 813227

Farm & Country Holidays
Home Farm
Norbury
Ashbourne DE6 2ED
☎ (0335) 324284

Peak District Farm Holidays
Lydgate Farm
Aldwark
Grangemill
Wirksworth DE4 4HD
☎ (0629) 85250

Information Centre
Town Hall, Market Place
Macclesfield SK10 1HR
☎ (0625) 504114

Youth Hostels

There are a number of youth hostels in the Peak District. You may join the Youth Hostels Association at the hostel, and it is advisable to book in advance to ensure a bed. Family accommodation is available at some hostels throughout the year and at the warden's discretion at other hostels.

There are youth hostels at Bakewell, Bretton, Buxton, Castleton, Crowden, Dimmingsdale (Oakamoor), Edale, Elton, Eyam, Gradbach, Hartington, Hathersage, Ilam, Langsett, Matlock, Meerbrook, Ravenstor near Miller's Dale, Shining Cliff near Ambergate and Youlgreave. Field Study facilities are available at Eyam, Hartington, Ilam and Gradbach hostels.

Further details are available from:

YHA Peak Area Office
PO Box 11, Unit 5 Tor Mill,
Dimple Road, Matlock, Derbys
☎ Matlock (0629) 825850

Camping Barns

The Peak National Park have encouraged the convertion of a number of traditional stone barns into basic low-cost overnight shelter — rather like a stone tent, but with the advantages of weatherproof roof and room to move about! You sleep on a wooden platform, there is a cooking area, table and benches, toilet and a water supply. You are expected to provide all the usual camping equipment, apart from a tent. Those under 18 years old must be accompanied by an adult, and strictly no dogs. There are camping barns at Edale, Upper Booth (Edale), Losehill (Castleton), Abney, Bakewell, One Ash Grange (Monyash), Birchover, Nab End (Hollinsclough), Warslow, Butterton (2), Old Glossop and Taddington. Full details, including how to book, are given in a leaflet obtainable from the Peak National Park.

Camping & Caravanning

There are a large number of sites for both tents and caravans. Details can be obtained from the Peak National Park and local tourist information offices.

Cycle Hire

Tissington Trail & High Peak Trail

Bikes may be hired from both Ashbourne and Parsley Hay station sites. The latter is situated just north of the old Hartington Station. Also Middleton Top Engine House. There is usually no need to book except for parties.

Mapleton Lane, Ashbourne
☎ 0335 343156
For Tissington Trail

Middleton Top
☎ 0629 823204
For High Peak Trail

Parsley Hay
On A515 Ashbourne-Buxton road
☎ 0298 484493
For both Tissington and High Peak Trails

Manifold Valley Light Railway Trail (Hamps & Mainfold Valleys)

Hire centre in old railway goods shed at rear of the Crown Inn, Waterhouses. Cycles may be also hired from Brown End Farm at the entrance to the tarmac-surfaced track.

Old Station carpark, Waterhouses
☎ 0538 308609
Open: March to October

Sett Valley Trail
Hayfield
☎ 0633 746222
Open: July-September daily
approx 9.30am-6pm, rest of
year weekends and bank
holidays.

Other cycle hire

Derwent Reservoir
☎ Hope Valley (0433) 651261
Approx 2 miles north of
Ashopton viaduct.

Monsal Head Cycle Hire
Monsal Head, Bakewell
☎ Gt Longstone (062 987) 505
or Tideswell (0298) 871679
Open: April-September,
daily, 9.30am-7pm; October-
March, normally open every
day except Christmas Day,
but telephone in advance for
midweek useage.

Fishing

Game Fishing

Certain hotels have rights available for guests. These include:

Baslow
Cavendish Hotel
☎ Baslow (0246) 582311
River Wye: three rods,
Cressbrook Mill to Ashford
(approx 4½ miles).
River Derwent: three rods,
Calver Bridge, east side, and
St Mary's Wood, west side,
down to Smelting Mill
Bridge, Rowsley (6½ miles).
Brown trout are restocked
annually from Chatsworth's
ponds, rainbow trout and
grayling breed naturally.

Dovedale
Izaak Walton Hotel
☎ Thorpe Cloud (033 529) 555

Matlock
The Midland Hotel
☎ Matlock (0629) 582630
River Derwent from Hall
Leys Park, Matlock to
Cromford.

Rowsley
Grouse & Claret
☎ Darley Dale (0629) 733233

Peacock Hotel
☎ (0629) 3518
Trout: 7 miles of River Wye.
Grayling: 2 miles of river
Derwent.

The National Park issues a leaflet on fishing in its *Fact Finder*
series.

Reservoir Fishing

For permission to fish the area's reservoirs contact the appropri-
ate water authority.

Derwent Reservoir
Ladybower Reservoir
Severn Trent Water Ltd,
(North Derbys District),
43 Dimple Road,
Matlock,
Derbys
☎ (0629) 55051

Tittesworth Reservoir
(also bird watching)
Severn Trent Water Ltd,
(Stoke District),
Westport Road,
Burslem,
Stoke-on-Trent,
Staffs
☎ (0538) 300389

Damflask Reservoir
Yorkshire Water Services Ltd,
Conservation & Recreation,
West Riding House,
67 Albion Street,
Leeds LS1 5AA

Rudyard Lake
British Waterways Board,
Reservoir Attendant,
Reservoir Cottage,
Rudyard Lake, Leek, Staffs
☎ (0538)33280

Bottoms,Errwood, Lamaload,
Ridgegate, Teggsnose &
Valehouse Reservoirs
North West Water Authority,
New Town House,
Buttermarket Street,
Warrington, Cheshire

Picnic Sites

W/C = toilet facilities available
W/C-d = toilet facilities for the disabled also available

With tables & seats:

Ashbourne, Mapleton Lane: SK175469
Blore Pasture (overlooks Dovedale): SK136498 W/C
Butterley Hill, Tansley Moor: SK349598 W/C
Calton Lees, near Chatsworth: SK258685 W/C
Cromford Meadows: SK300571
Curbar Gap: SK263747
Darley Dale: SK270624
Derbyshire Bridge, Goyt Valley: SK017718 W/C-d
Derwent Reservoir: SK173893 Fairholmes Cycle Hire Centre W/C-d
Edale, Barber Booth: SK107847
Errwood Reservoir, Goyt Valley: SK012748 and SK012731. A toilet
    (W/C-d) has been built at the eastern end of Errwood Dam.
Froghall Canal Wharf: SK027478 W/C
Goyts Clough Quarry, Goyt Valley: SK012735 W/C

Hayfield (former station) on Sett Valley Trail: SK035869 W/C-d
High Peak Trail:
    Friden: SK173607
    Minninglow: SK195582
    Middleton Top Engine House: SK276552 W/C
    Black Rocks: SK291557 W/C
    High Peak Junction: SK313560 W/C
Ilam Hall: SK132507 W/C-d (female only). Information centre, café.
Lamaload Reservoir: SK975753 W/C
Longshaw Lodge: SK266802 W/C-d. Information centre (National Trust), café.
Lyme Park: SJ963825 W/C (National Trust)
Mam Nick, Rushup Edge: SK124833
Matlock Moor, SK324633
Moor Lane, Youlgreave: SK194645
Oakamoor, on site of old copper works: SK053448 W/C
Over Haddon: SK204664 W/C-d
Saddleworth, Binn Green: SK030065 W/C
Stanage, Hollin Bank: SK237838 W/C-d
Tegg's Nose, nr Macclesfield Forest: SJ950733 W/C. Information centre.
Tideswell Dale: SK154742 W/C
Tissington Trail:
    Mapleton Lane: SK175469 Water for horses
    Thorpe: SK165503 Shelter (no picnic tables)
    Tissington: SK177521 W/C-d
    Alsop-en-le-Dale: SK156549 Shelter
    Hartington: SK150611 W/C Information centre
    Parsley Hay: SK147636 W/C-d
    Hurdlow: SK127659
Tittesworth Reservoir, Meerbrook: SJ994603 W/C. Children's play area.
Torside: SK067983 W/C-d
Waterhouses: SK085502 W/C-d
White Lodge, Monsal Dale: SK171706 W/C

No tables and seats, but off-the-road car parking available:
Alstonfield: SK131556 W/C
Ashford-in-the-Water: SK215768 W/C-d

Baslow: SK260720 W/C
Baslow Edge: SK261748
Castleton: SK149829 W/C-d
Cisterns Clough, Axe Edge: SK034698
Elton Common: SK226598
Hathersage: SK232814 W/C
Hope: SK170835 W/C
Hulme End: SK104594
Longnor Village: SK089649 W/C
Matlock Bath railway station (adjoining): SK298584 W/C
Matlock Dale (nr High Tor): SK297595 W/C Fishing
Monsal Head: SK185715 W/C
Rudyard Lake: SJ951583 W/C Public slipway
Thorpe Village: SK156505 W/C-d
Weag's Bridge, Manifold Valley: SK100542
Wetton: SK109553 W/C-d
Wetton Mill, Manifold Valley: SK096561 Café. W/C. Café has
    tables for patrons, but main car park does not.

Public Transport

There are bus services along most of the major roads across or around the Peak District, but rural services are infrequent or non-existent. Without an annual subsidy of £70,000 from the Peak National Park Board bus and rail services would be much worse than they are.

The main InterCity trains from London stop at Derby, Chesterfield and Sheffield, all of which are convenient for the eastern side of the Peak District. On the western side there are trains from London to Stoke-on-Trent and Manchester via Macclesfield. The only cross-Peak railway line is between Manchester and Sheffield along the Hope Valley line, with stations at Disley, Chinley, Edale, Hope, Bamford, Hathersage and Grindleford. Trains also run from Manchester to both Buxton and Glossop, and from Derby to Matlock, stopping at stations en route.

If you are proposing visiting the Peak using public transport enquire at the nearest tourist information office to your destination for details of local services.

Riding Stables

Curbar Edge Riding School
'Emberbrook',
Bar Road, Curbar,
Calver, Sheffield S30 1YA
☎ Hope Valley (0433) 30584

Endon Riding School
Coltslow Farm,
Stanley Moss Lane,
Stockton Brook,
near Stoke-on-Trent
☎ (0782) 502114

Hopkin Farm
Tansley
☎ Matlock (0629) 582253

Lady Booth Riding Centre
Edale
☎ Hope Valley (0433) 670205

Northfield Farm
Flash, near Buxton
☎ Buxton (0298) 22543

Red House Stables
Old Road,
Darley Dale
☎ Matlock (0629) 733583

Rushup Hall
Chapel-en-le-Frith
☎ (0298) 3323

Spring Paddock Riding School
Marple Road,
Charlesworth,
Hyde
☎ Glossop (0457) 853175

Sailing

Where sailing is allowed on reservoirs the relevant water authority has delegated responsibility for the sailing on that water to various clubs. In some cases these clubs allow casual visitors and it is necessary to write to the club if you wish to sail there.

Bottoms Lodge Reservoir
Glossop & District Sailing Club
Mrs R. Mason,
23 Edale Close,
Hazelgrove,
Stockport, Cheshire

Combs Reservoir
Details from:
North West Water,
Rivers Division,
Buttermarket Street,
Warrington, Cheshire

Damflask Reservoir
Sheffield Viking Sailing Club
Mr A. J. Pemberton,
41 Chelsea Road,
Sheffield 11

Dove Stones Reservoir
Dove Stones Sailing Club
Mr J. Ball,
28 Dorset Avenue,
High Crompton,
Shaw,
Lancs

Errwood Reservoir
Errwood Sailing Club
Mr A. Gay,
Four Oaks, The Coppice,
Higher Poynton, Cheshire

Rudyard Lake
Casual visitors should contact:
Reservoir Attendant,
Reservoir Cottage,
Rudyard Lake, Leek

Torside Reservoir
Glossop Sailing Club
Mrs R. Mason,
23 Edale Close,
Hazelgrove,
Stockport,
Cheshire

Shows, Well Dressing & Local Events

There are many activities going on in the area and the list below includes the majority of those occuring annually. Some events occur over the end of one month and the beginning of the next and are listed twice. It is important to realise that there are many events which are not included but which may be of interest. Readily springing to mind are the occasional steaming days at Leawood Pump House, festivals at Haddon Hall; local village events such as church festivals; talks and organised rambles.

A full list of events is published in the free newspaper, *Peakland Post*, published by the National Park and available from information centres or from the National Park Office (enclose a stamped addressed envelope).

Early spring
Ashbourne Shrovetide
   Football: Shrove Tuesday
   and Ash Wednesday.
Flagg Races (High Peak Hunt
   Point to Point): Tuesday
   after Easter

May
Alstonfield Horse Show and
   Gymkhana
Ashford-in-the-Water Well
   Dressing
Bamford Sheep Dog Trials
Castleton Garland Ceremony:
   28 May (Oak Apple Day)

Chatsworth Angling Fair
Endon Well Dressing
Etwall Well Dressing
Leek Arts Festival
Leek May Fair
Middleton-by-Youlgreave
   Well Dressing
Monyash Well Dressing
Pott Shrigley Rose Queen Fête
Tissington Well Dressing:
   Ascension Day until
   following Monday
Winster Market Fair: Bank
   Holiday Monday
Wirksworth Well Dressing

June

Ashford-in-the-Water Well
  Dressing
Chelmorton Well Dressing
Grindleford Carnival
Hope Well Dressing and
  Wakes
Litton Well Dressing
Monyash Well Dressing
Rowsley Well Dressing and
  Festival
Tideswell Well Dressing and
  Wakes Carnival
Winster Wakes
Youlgreave Well Dressing

June-July

Bakewell Well Dressing and
  Carnival week including
  raft race on River Wye

July

Alport Love Feast
Ashbourne Carnival
Ashbourne Highland
  Gathering
Bamford Carnival
Baslow Well Dressing
Bradwell Well Dressing and
  Gala week
Buxton International Arts
  Festival
Buxton Well Dressing
Chesterfield Medieval Market
Glossop Carnival
Hollinsclough village fête
Hope Well Dressing and
  Wakes
Leek Club Day (Sunday
  School and other organisa-
  tions procession)

Leek Show
Litton Well Dressing
Lyme Park Festival
Padley Pilgrimage
Pilsley Well Dressing
Stoney Middleton Well
  Dressing
Tideswell Well Dressing
Winster Wakes

August

Ashbourne Show
Ashover Show
Bakewell Show
Bradwell Well Dressing and
  Gala week
Chesterfield Market: Bank
  Holiday
Crich Tramway Museum,
  Grand Transport Extrava-
  ganza
Cromford Steam Rally
Dovedale Sheepdog Trials
Eyam Well Dressing
Foolow Well Dressing
Froggatt Show
Grindleford Show
Hope Show
Hucklow and District Wakes
Ipstones Show
Leek Carnival
Lyme Park Festival
Lyme Sheepdog Trials
Macclesfield Forest Chapel
  Rush Bearing
Manifold Valley Show
Wormhill Well Dressing

September

Chatsworth Country Fair

Eyam Well Dressing
Foolow Well Dressing
Hartington Sports
Hartington Well Dressing
Holme Valley Torchlight Procession
Jenkin Chapel, Saltersford Harvest Thanksgiving
Longnor Well Dressing and Sports
Longshaw Sheepdog Trials
Lyme Park Horse Trials '
Matlock Bath Illuminations and Firework Display
Penistone Show
Wormhill Well Dressing

Sports & Outdoor Activities

Caving

The many caves and mines should never be entered by the inexperienced. Two useful addresses are:

Derbyshire Caving Association
c/o The Sports Council,
East Midlands Regional Office,
Grove House,
Bridgeford Road,
West Bridgeford,
Nottingham NG2 6AP

Peak District Mines Historical Society,
c/o Peak District Mining Museum,
The Pavilion
Matlock Bath.
☎ (0629) 583834

Cave Rescue

In an emergency dial 999 and ask for Cave Rescue.

Gliding

The Derbyshire and Lancashire Gliding Club
Camphill, Great Hucklow
☎ Buxton (0298) 871270/871207
Details of membership, holiday courses etc are available from the club manager. In addition to the clubhouse, facilities include overnight accommodation, a full catering service and children's playground. The club currently owns five two-seater and four single-seater gliders.

Walking

Walking is the most popular outdoor activity as the Peak District has walks of all grades of difficulty and length, in fascinating and varied scenery. Many walks are described in this book, or plan your own route with the aid of a large scale OS map. Wear boots or stout shoes (especially on the moors), take weatherproof chlothing and a map (and know how to read it correctly).

For those who prefer a guided tour the National Trust provides a series of 'Walks with a Ranger' throughout the Peak District. Booking by telephone is essential. Details from :
National Trust, High Peak Estate Office
☎ Hope Valley (0433) 670368

Squash Courts
There are squash courts at Ashbourne; Callow Park, Wirksworth; Leek; Glossop; Sheffield; and Cressbrook Mill, Monsal Dale.

Swimming Pools
There are pools at Leek, Cheadle, Ashbourne, Buxton, Glossop, Matlock and Chesterfield, plus an open-air swimming pool at Hathersage with heated and filtered water, open May to mid-September (closed Sunday).

Tourist Information Centres

Details of local information centres are given in the Additional Information at the end of each chapter.

Peak National Park
Head Office, Aldern House, Baslow Road, Bakewell, Derbys DE4 1AE
☎ Bakewell (0629) 814321
The National Park also run a wide range of residential courses at Losehill Hall. For details write to:
Peak National Park Study Centre,
Losehill Hall, Castleton, Derbys S30 2WB
☎ Hope Valley (0433) 620373

National Trust
East Midlands Regional Office,
Clumber Stableyard, Worksop,
Notts S80 3BE
☎ Worksop (0909) 486411

Regional Tourist Boards
Due to an odd quirk of administration four different regional tourist boards cover the Peak District:

East Midlands Tourist Board
Exchequergate,
Lincoln LN2 1PZ
☎ (0522) 31521

Heart of England Tourist Board
Woodside, Larkhill Road, Worcester WR5 2EF

Yorkshire and Humberside Tourist Board
312 Tadcaster Road, York
☎ York (0904) 707961

North West Tourist Board
The Last Drop Village,
Bromley Cross, Bolton, Lancs
☎ Bolton (0204) 591511

INDEX

A Note to the Reader

Thank you for buying this book, we hope it has helped you to enjoy your visit to the Peak District. We have worked hard to produce a guidebook which is as accurate as possible. With this in mind, any comments, suggestions or useful information you may have would be appreciated.

Please send your letters to:
The Editor
Moorland Publishing Co Ltd
Moor Farm Road West
Ashbourne
Derbyshire
DE6 1HD

MPC The Travel Specialists

Visitor's Guides

Tour & Explore with MPC Visitor's Guides

Regional Traveller

The user-friendly itinerary-based guides to give you the best in sightseeing and practical information

Athens & Peleponnese

Austria

Austria: Tyrol &
  Vorarlberg

Britain:

Cornwall & Isles of Scilly

Cotswolds

Devon

East Anglia

Hampshire & Isle of Wight

Kent

Lake District

Scotland: Lowlands

Somerset, Dorset & Wiltshire

North Wales & Snowdonia

North York Moors, York &
  Coast

Northumbria

Northern Ireland

Peak District

Treasure Houses of England

Yorkshire Dales & North
  Pennines

Denmark

Egypt

France:

Alps & Jura

Brittany

Dordogne

Loire

Massif Central

Normandy

Normany Landing Beaches

Northeast France

Provence & Côte d'Azur

Germany:

Bavaria

Black Forest

Rhine & Mosel

Southern Germany

Northern Germany

Italy:

Florence & Tuscany

Italian Lakes

Northern Italy

Southern Italy

Spain:
Costa Brava to Costa
   Blanca
Northern & Central Spain
Southern Spain & Costa
   del Sol

Switzerland
Turkey
USA
California
Florida
Orlando & Central Florida

Holiday Islands
**Explore your holiday island, experience the local
atmosphere, see all the sights — and the best beaches**

Corsica
Crete
Cyprus
Guernsey, Alderney & Sark
Jersey
Sardinia
Madeira

Mallorca, Menorca,
   Ibiza & Formentera
Malta & Gozo
Mauritius, Rodrigues &
   Reunion
Tenerife

Country Traveller
The larger format Visitor's Guides

Canada
Czechoslovakia
France
Greece
Holland
Hungary

Iceland & Greenland
Norway
Portugal
Sweden
USA

**A complete catalogue of all MPC travel guides
is available on request**